TIME

D-DAY

24 Hours That Saved the World

D-DAY: 24 Hours That Saved the World

MANAGING EDITOR	Kelly Knauer
DESIGNER	Ellen Fanning
PICTURE EDITOR	Patricia Cadley
WRITER/RESEARCH DIRECTOR	Matthew McCann Fenton
COPY EDITOR	Bruce Christopher Carr
GRAPHICS	Jackson Dykman, Joe Lertola, Lon Tweeten
RESEARCH	Rudi Papiri

TIME INC. HOME ENTERTAINMENT

PRESIDENT	Rob Gursha
VICE PRESIDENT, BRANDED BUSINESSES	David Arfine
VICE PRESIDENT, NEW PRODUCT DEVELOPMENT	Richard Fraiman
EXECUTIVE DIRECTOR, MARKETING SERVICES	Carol Pittard
DIRECTOR, RETAIL & SPECIAL SALES	Tom Mifsud
DIRECTOR OF FINANCE	Tricia Griffin
ASSISTANT MARKETING DIRECTOR	Ann Marie Doherty
PREPRESS MANAGER	Emily Rabin
BOOK PRODUCTION MANAGER	Jonathan Polsky
MARKETING MANAGER	Sara Stumpf

SPECIAL THANKS TO:

Bozena Bannett; Alex Bliss; Bernadette Corbie; Robert Dente; Gina Di Meglio; Julius Domone; Anne-Michelle Gallero; Sara Gootee; Peter Harper; Suzanne Janso; Ralph K. Manley; Robert Marasco; Natalie McCrea; Mary Jane Rigoroso; Steven Sandonato; Vincent Schlotterbeck; Mark A. Schmidt, The Museum of WW II; Grace Sullivan; Paula Ussery, The National D-Day Museum; Cornelis Verwaal; Louise Whall

A NOTE ON SOURCES

This book celebrates all the soldiers of D-day: not just the colorful commanders but also the quartermasters, engineers, naval officers, medics and others whose significant contributions to the success of Operation Overlord are often overlooked. To tell their stories, we looked first in the pages of TIME and LIFE from 1944. Here we found not only the expected riches, like the historic and well-known photos of Robert Capa, but also unique eyewitness accounts of the invasion of Normandy—reporting that remains as fresh and moving as the day it was written. Two of the chapters in this book, on the worldwide re-action to D-day and on the liberation of Paris, are taken verbatim from 1944 issues of TIME. We have also relied on TIME's re-porting in the months and years following D-day, including numerous interviews with participants in the landings.

Like every reader, scholar or editor exploring D-day, we have often turned to two classic works of reporting, Cornelius Ryan's *The Longest Day* (1959) and Stephen Ambrose's *D-Day June 6, 1944* (1994). We have borrowed a few anecdotes from their pages, have acknowledged their provenance when doing so, and heartily recommend these volumes to readers. We can also recommend recent works on D-day by Will Fowler and Dan Van Der Vat, as well as Gerald Astor's *June 6, 1944: The Voices of D-Day*, a fine oral history. The thorough volumes on D-day in Osprey Publishing's *Campaign* series will especially appeal to armchair generals. We would also like to acknowledge the contributions of the National D-Day Museum in New Orleans and the Museum of World War II in Natick, Mass., whose curators have graciously shared the historic artifacts featured in these pages. Those seeking a closer encounter with D-day will profit from a visit to these two institutions.

—The Editors

First Edition • ISBN: 1-932273-22-0 • Library of Congress Control Number: 2003114085

TIME is a trademark of Time Inc.

We welcome your comments and suggestions about TIME Books. Please write to us at TIME Books • Attention: Book Editors • PO Box 11016 • Des Moines, IA 50336-1016

If you would like to order any of our hardcover Collector's Edition books, please call us at 1-800-327-6388. (Monday through Friday, 7 a.m.–8 p.m., or Saturday, 7 a.m.–6 p.m., Central time)

PRINTED IN THE UNITED STATES OF AMERICA

TIME

D-DAY

24 Hours That Saved the World

OLD GLORY: This flag, carried into action on D-day, is on display from the National D-Day Museum in New Orleans

By the Editors of TIME

Contents

H-HOUR, D-DAY: American soldiers charge ashore at Omaha Beach in the first wave of the landings. This is one of the few pictures taken by LIFE photographer Robert Capa in that desperate hour that survived

ROBERT CAPA—MAGNUM PHOTOS

Cover: Background Photo: National Archives. Insets (L to R): Topham—The Image Works; David E. Scherman—Time Life Pictures; U.S. Army—AP/Wide World; Corbis; U.S. Army Signal Corps; Frank Scherschel—Time Life Pictures

LEST WE FORGET: Tom Hanks speaks at the dedication ceremony for the National D-Day Museum in New Orleans on June 6, 2000

Imagine If...

By Tom Hanks

IMAGINE IF D-DAY HAD BEEN A CATASTROPHIC FAILURE FOR the Allies. Say that on June 6, 1944, American soldiers had failed to take the bluffs at Omaha Beach, stranding them in nothing less than a killing field. Allied landing craft, the very same boats that had deposited the soldiers at dawn, would have had to make their way ashore once again to evacuate those who survived the murderous fire from the enemy. The Nazi war machine, including *Ost* Battalion troops from nations long since swallowed up by Adolf Hitler's Third Reich, would have successfully repelled the invaders along that critical stretch of northern France.

Then, imagine the Americans at Utah Beach having no other force to join. The German army, having defeated the Americans once already, would have had more troops and more incentive to wage battle. What would have happened to the Allied plan to cut off the Cotentin Peninsula from Nazi-occupied France and make the city of Cherbourg a secure port and the main artery for incoming Allied forces and matériel?

Say, too, that the British forces at beaches code-named

Gold and Sword had been surprised not only by severe seas and a tide that rose too high, too fast but also by the Luftwaffe. Imagine if the sky had been stacked with enemy aircraft attacking the landing force, refueling, rearming and attacking again. What if the German forces being held in reserve to take on what was thought to be the main invasion point, at Calais, had instead been moved forward to attack and ensnare the British Tommies within yards of the Normandy coastline?

What if the Canadians, after landing at Juno Beach, had been the only Allied force to penetrate the French countryside ? They would still have found themselves in the *Bocage,* the French farmland quilted with hedgerows taller and deeper than expected, natural barriers so dense as to be practically impenetrable. With an invasion force only one-fifth the size planned in Operation Overlord, how long would it have been before Hitler's "Fortress Europe" proved itself unconquerable or, at the least, safe from invasion on that long day?

What if the war in Europe had been prolonged? A year or more might have passed before the Allies could regroup, replenish, retrain, replan and reinvade northern Europe. Without having to defend a western front, imagine the advantages the Wehrmacht would have enjoyed against the Soviet Union. And how much stronger would Germany have been against the Allied forces fighting in Italy, who liberated Rome on the seldom-celebrated date of June 5, 1944? Consider the horrors the Nazi regime could have committed had the Holocaust lasted 12 months longer. Envision cities other than Hiroshima and Nagasaki that could have been targets of the atomic weapons the U.S. brought into the world in the summer of 1945.

WHAT *IF* D-DAY HAD FAILED? IN FACT, IT NEARLY DID. THE success of Operation Overlord came despite a myriad of mistakes and unworkable plans. Landings were made miles off target; tanks that were supposed to be amphibious sank to the bottom of the English Channel, killing their crews before they could fire a shot. Much of the air support the invading forces were told would soften up their landing areas did more damage to cow pastures than to enemy positions. Many of the paratroopers had their weapons and gear stripped off their bodies by the force of their jumps and landed nowhere near their targets. The Army Rangers who fought their way up the defended cliffs of Pointe du Hoc to destroy German heavy artillery initially found that the guns they came to destroy were not even in position.

June 6, 1944, ended with few achieved goals and thousands of dead and wounded troops. Most of the Allied forces—the liberators who had been in France for less than a day—were crouching, marching or fighting far from where they were supposed to be.

And yet the invasion—the largest and most complicated in the history of the world—was a success. The willingness of the soldiers, sailors and airmen to confront the enemy on that

Day of Days made it so. To paraphrase Dwight Eisenhower in his interview with Walter Cronkite on the 20th anniversary of the invasion, the junior officers improvised, the NCOs kept driving forward, the weaponless soldiers picked up rifles, someone got up above the beach, others followed—and the invasion carried on.

Men took heroic actions in Normandy that literally saved the day. Many struggled just to live to see June 7 and, by doing so, helped guarantee success. Those who toiled far away from the battle—at airfields, on ships, in basements, offices and hospitals, in jobs as mundane as operating telephones and filling gasoline drums—helped save Operation Overlord as well.

Some never got the chance to do what was expected of them—the men who drowned in the Channel, were killed on the beaches or lost their lives in the farmlands. Yet the names etched in stone above their earthly remains provide evidence of their contributions. Those who simply *disappeared*, their bodies and souls having vanished in the haze and hell of the battle on June 6, must be credited in absentia.

They are all responsible for the success of Operation Overlord. Their efforts and sacrifices are why—as one American newspaper stated—the world as we would know it for decades to come was decided in the fields and beaches of Normandy.

FOR THE 50TH ANNIVERSARY OF D-DAY IN 1994, MICHELIN reissued a special guide that had been prepared in 1949, the fifth anniversary of the invasion. Outdated by 45 years when republished, and now by 55 years, the map is a telling and evocative guide to the tragedy and triumph evident across the countryside of northern France. In 1949, cemeteries were scattered abundantly throughout the landscape. The wreckage of war—skeletal, rusting vehicles, downed aircraft and destroyed tanks from both the Allies and the enemy—was everywhere. Scars on the earth were plainly visible and would be for years to come. Many of the concrete bunkers and barracks of the occupying force were still there, just as they still are.

There are also dates on the reissued map. Each village is marked with the day, in 1944, when Allied forces took the town, liberating the people who had been living under Nazi domination since 1940. It is possible to stand in one small French town and see the steeple of a church in another village just a few kilometers away. Looking at the map, you can see that the village you were standing in was freed on, say, June 9. The village in the distance was not taken until the first week of July. The two towns were separated by a few minutes' drive in 1949, as they are in 2004. But in the early summer of 1944, that same short distance measured the void between freedom and tyranny—a void that was bridged by the timeless, soul-wrenching exhaustion of combat, blood and death.

What one can often forget about June 6, 1944, is that it was only 24 hours long. Before peace was to come to the peoples of Europe, before the English, Canadian, American and all the other Allied forces could go back to their homes, 336 more days would have to pass—many of them just as deadly and dangerous as that one day in June. What we must remember about D-day is that the peace that was unconditionally won in World War II would not have happened without that longest of days. ∎

COURTESY NATIONAL D-DAY MUSEUM

The National D-Day Museum

The National D-Day Museum in New Orleans opened its doors on June 6, 2000, and has now welcomed more than 1 million visitors. Many of the Artifacts featured in this volume are part its permanent collection. In 2003 the U.S. Congress designated the Museum "America's National World War II Museum." Its popularity has sparked an ambitious expansion campaign, now under way, that will triple its size and allow it to feature artifacts, exhibits, films and other source materials covering all of the campaigns and service branches that played a role in World War II. The expansion will also create the Center for the Study of the American Spirit, which will foster educational inquiry into the war and its lasting influences and will generate outreach programs for America's schools.

Tom Hanks, who starred in the 1998 film *Saving Private Ryan*, is a longtime supporter of efforts to honor the veterans of World War II and to celebrate the ideals for which they fought. As the honorary chairman of the National D-Day Museum's capital campaign, he invites readers of this volume to visit the Museum or its website (*www.ddaymuseum.org*) and to contribute to the $150 million expansion campaign.

For more information, or to contribute, please contact:
The National D-Day Museum
945 Magazine Street
New Orleans, LA 70130
(504) 527-6012 (ext. 329)

NORMANDY, 1944

" The destruction of the enemy's landing is the sole decisive factor in the whole conduct of the war and hence in its final results."

—Adolf Hitler

Fortress Europe

In 1941 Adolf Hitler dominated Europe. Three years later, his empire was crumbling—and, at last, the Allies were preparing to strike back

JUNE 1941: ADOLF HITLER REIGNED AS EUROPE'S MASTER. It was an incredible achievement. Less than ten years before, the Austrian-born World War I veteran had tricked and blustered his way into the leadership of a penniless and disarmed Germany. Now, from the Pyrenees to the Arctic Circle, from Normandy to Warsaw to Crete, the Nazi dictator ruled virtually unchallenged over more of Europe than any one man had governed since the days of the Roman Empire. And his friends and allies ruled in Moscow, Tokyo, Rome, Madrid. His only remaining enemy, Britain, was badly mauled and begging for U.S. supplies. Yet Americans remained strictly neutral and isolationist, even if most favored the British. Besides, the U.S. was pitifully weak: it boasted an Army of barely three divisions and an Air Force of some 300 fighters.

That same month—June 1941—Hitler attacked his "ally," Soviet Russia. The decision sealed his doom. Three years later, in June 1944, the Germans were on the defensive. Hitler's armies were bogged down in Russia. In Africa his panzers had been defeated by British and U.S. forces. His divisions were now engaged in Italy, fighting a bitter holding battle along the spine of the peninsula against tenacious Allied armies. And in England, his enemies were harnessing the vast supplies of armaments produced in America—now President Franklin D. Roosevelt's "arsenal of democracy"—and were preparing to launch the long dreamed-of invasion of occupied France.

That invasion, D-day, is the subject of this book, and to understand its importance, we must review the events that brought the world's great nations to this fateful hour.

In the five years from 1936 to 1941, Hitler's armies—and his diplomats—had rolled over Europe. In 1936 Germany violated the terms of the Treaty of Versailles and reoccupied the Rhineland; the Western powers did nothing. That same year Hitler signed a pact with equally imperialist and militarist

WAITING: A German soldier guards the Normandy coast in 1944. Anticipating a major seaborne invasion by the Allies, Hitler—who had conquered France by rolling around its vaunted defense, the Maginot Line—now committed himself to a defensive strategy. He poured resources into making the French coast impregnable

GRAPHIC PHOTO UNION

GETAWAY: The Anglo-British army was bottled up in Dunkirk in 1940, but Hitler, for reasons unknown, held his panzers in check, allowing a massive evacuation. The curious decision would be echoed in Normandy four years later, when Hitler again held back his tanks

Japan. In March 1938 Hitler seized Austria. In September he enticed Britain's idealistic Prime Minister Neville Chamberlain to Munich, where the Sudetenland of Czechoslovakia was ceded to Germany as the price of "peace for our time." With memories of World War I still running deep, the leaders of Western Europe pursued the policy of appeasement with pride, committed to negotiating with Hitler rather than fighting him.

In March 1939 Hitler occupied the rest of Czechoslovakia. In April he made territorial demands on Poland, and Britain threatened war. On Aug. 23 Hitler's Nazi Germany and Stalin's Marxist-Leninist Russia, previously bitter enemies, agreed to sign a nonaggression pact. Only one week later, with his eastern flank now secure, Hitler launched a blitzkrieg (lightning attack) on Poland, propelling Europe into war.

A series of incredible victories followed: German troops crushed Poland, easily rolled over Norway, the Balkans and the Netherlands, then surged past the "impenetrable" Maginot Line to conquer France. In June 1940, the main Anglo-French army was cut off, encircled by German armies at the Belgian port of Dunkirk. For reasons still not fully understood, Hitler halted his panzer divisions, allowing the Allied force—almost 350,000 soldiers—to be safely evacuated. That bungled decision

would later return to haunt him.

Through the summer of 1940, Hitler contemplated an invasion of Britain, dubbed Operation Sea Lion. In fact, the Germans did not even have enough ships to ferry the 90,000 soldiers envisioned for the invasion across the English Channel, much less the 170,000 more troops slated to follow in two days. But Hitler's air force, the Luftwaffe, controlled the skies, and the Germans decided to bomb England—now led by Hitler's ardent foe, Winston Churchill—into submission and surrender.

Adlertag (Eagle Day) was the name for the first massive bombing raids on Aug. 13, 1940. Some 1,500 Luftwaffe warplanes swept across R.A.F. airfields in southeast England, badly damaging five of them and knocking out one. The next day the Luftwaffe was back, then the day after, and so began the Battle of Britain, the first ever to be fought entirely in the skies. German Air Marshal Hermann Göring had roughly 1,400 bombers and nearly 1,000 fighters, the R.A.F. defenders fewer than 900 fighters. The outnumbered British fought with a kind of desperation that inspired Churchill to say of them, "Never in the field of human conflict was so much owed by so many to so few." The British weathered Hitler's airborne blitz, though it continued into the spring of 1941. Some 30,000 British lives were lost, but the essential result was that for the

Hitler's Empire June 6, 1944

300 mi.
300 km

- ◼ Axis-dominated area
- ◻ Neutral countries
- ▨ Area under Allied control
- ▨ Area formerly under Axis control

INP—CORBIS

MASTER OF PARIS: France and Britain declared war on Germany in September 1939, following Hitler's invasion of Poland. After a calm winter, German armies subdued France in only six weeks in the spring of 1940. On June 23, the Führer visited the conquered City of Light. With only a day to spare, he claimed he was just another harassed tourist

JUNE 1940

first time, Hitler's military had been beaten completely stymied.

The virus of war now infected new fronts. An outnumbered British army beat off an attempt by Hitler's Axis partner, Italian strongman Benito Mussolini, to seize the Suez Canal. Hitler sent one of his ablest tank commanders, General Erwin Rommel, to rescue the Italians in North Africa, and "the Desert Fox" pushed the weakened British back into Egypt.

In the Balkans, meanwhile, a British-backed coup overthrew the pro-German government of Yugoslavia in March 1941. Hitler was so angered that he decided almost overnight to invade, and he conquered his prey in about a week. While he was at it, he took over a bungled Italian invasion of Greece and subdued that country in less than a month.

HITLER'S POWER WAS NOW AT ITS HEIGHT. BUT IN THIS moment of supreme triumph, in the spring of 1941, he boldly made the error that was to destroy him: he decided to invade his ally of convenience, Soviet Russia. Exactly why he made this catastrophic miscalculation may never be known. In part it was ideology. He had begun his political career by attacking the Bolsheviks, and he dreamed of Germany's finding *Lebensraum* (living room) by colonizing the vast lands to the east.

In part, too, it was a matter of paranoia. Hitler suspected that Churchill fought on largely because he hoped to inveigle Stalin into joining him. And Hitler was himself so treacherous that he could not believe Stalin was not planning to betray him. Stalin intensified those suspicions by his own aggressiveness: in the late spring of 1940, the Soviets seized the Baltic states of Latvia, Lithuania and Estonia, then demanded and got Romania to give up its provinces of Bessarabia in north-

ern Bukovina. Hitler saw this as a threat to his access to Rumania's rich oil fields.

Hitler was finally a victim of his own successes. He could not believe that backward Russia, which had had trouble subduing hapless Finland, could resist the German army, the Wehrmacht. Even before the Battle of Britain, Hitler wanted his generals to start planning an invasion of Russia for the fall of 1940. They managed to talk him into delaying it until the following May. Germany signed a trade agreement with the U.S.S.R. as late as January 1941, but a month earlier Hitler had told his commanders, "The German armed forces must be prepared to crush Soviet Russia in a quick campaign." The battle plan called for some 148 divisions—more than 3 million men—to attack in three main drives along a 1,000-mile front. One army group would strike northward, toward Leningrad; another would move north of the Pripet Marshes toward Moscow, which Hitler planned to level and leave uninhabitable; a southern army, from Rumania, would storm across Ukraine toward Kiev and Stalingrad. "Operation Barbarossa," the Führer believed, would smash Russia within six months.

Hitler's impulsive attack on Yugoslavia in May 1941 delayed his invasion of Russia by a month—which was to become critically important when the first snows began to fall. But the Germans expected little trouble when they rescheduled Operation Barbarossa for June 22. They were right: despite major German troop movements, the supposedly crafty and suspi-

SNOWED UNDER: Outmanned, outfought and out in the cold, German troops trudge through the snow as they retreat from Moscow in the fall of 1941. Like Napoleon before him, Hitler was beaten not only by Russia's people but also by its vast size and its brutal weather

RUSSIA, 1941

cious Stalin foresaw nothing. When the Wehrmacht's panzers rolled, the Red Army was caught napping; hundreds of thousands of soldiers fell prisoner. Within three weeks the German line had moved forward some 400 miles, almost to Leningrad. But with the central army group in striking distance of Moscow, Hitler delayed its advance to concentrate on capturing Ukraine's industrial resources, and it was not until October that he began a new drive on the capital. Now the Soviets proved tougher than expected. The Germans originally estimated Soviet strength at about 200 divisions; Moscow eventually fielded some 400 divisions—roughly 6 million men.

Soon a cold rain began to fall; the first snows followed on Oct. 6. A month later, the temperatures fell below zero. Tank engines began to freeze. The troops, who had been issued no winter clothing, suffered frostbite. On Dec. 1 Hitler ordered the start of an all-out drive on Moscow, which the Wehrmacht now surrounded on three sides, only 20 to 30 miles outside the city. One infantry unit got as far as the suburb of Khimki, from which the Germans could actually see the towers of the Kremlin, but that was as far as they could go before Soviet tanks drove them out again. All along the front, the Soviet defenders held fast. Then, on Dec. 6, the Soviets somehow produced 100 new divisions and launched a furious counteroffensive that sent the Germans reeling back 50 miles by the end of the month. Moscow was saved. One day later, the Japanese bombed Pearl Harbor.

ONE OF THE FEW MEN OVERJOYED BY THAT BAD NEWS WAS Churchill. "So we had won after all," he thought on hearing it. "How long the war would last or in what fashion it would end no man could tell, nor did I at this moment care. Once again in our long island history, we should emerge, however mauled or mutilated, safe and victorious."

DESERT WAR: Australian tanks roll through Libya in 1941. The war in North Africa found the Germans and Allies trading victories under General Erwin Rommel and Britain's Field Marshal Bernard Montgomery. The German forces held out in Tunisia until 1943

America, he knew, was an ally whose massive resources could swing the pendulum of history against Hitler.

The America that entered the war was steeped in isolationism, and its cupboard of armaments was bare. So the year 1942 was devoted to holding actions in Europe, while U.S. Army Chief of Staff George C. Marshall began turning thousands of young farmers and laborers into soldiers, and industrialists like Henry Ford converted their auto assembly lines to churn out bombers. The war in the Pacific commanded the primary attention of the U.S. in 1942, as giant aircraft-carrier battles at Midway and the Coral Sea and the seaborne invasion of Guadalcanal halted Japan's previously unstoppable march of conquest in Asia.

But if all was quiet along Hitler's western front in 1942, his war in the east was sapping his strength. By March 1942, a Red Army offensive had pushed Hitler's front line in Russia back by 150 miles in some regions—at a cost of perhaps 4 million Russian lives. In June Hitler launched a major offensive in southern Russia, which culminated in the decisive Battle of Stalingrad. On Aug. 19 Field Marshal Friedrich von Paulus and some 300,000 German soldiers attacked the industrial city on the Volga River. In the next few months the city was destroyed in desperate house-to-house fighting. When Soviet reinforcements arrived in November, the Germans were trapped: they finally surrendered in January 1943. Later that year, German divisions were again repulsed by the Red Army

in a massive tank engagement, the Battle of Kursk. Somehow, Stalin and his defiant people had beaten back Hitler's invasion.

But the German empire could not be defeated on a single front. Since the first days of America's entry into the war, the need for a "second front" in Western Europe had been evident. Roosevelt and Churchill had persuaded Stalin to give them time to build up their forces before launching a major attack on Hitler's *Festung Europa*, his "Fortress Europe." In fact, the Allies directed several thrusts against Hitler's domain in 1942 and 1943. In November 1942, in Operation Torch, a mostly American force landed in the French colonies of Morocco, Algeria and Tunisia. Morocco and Algeria were soon under Allied control; but the Germans, under General Rommel, held off the Allied armies in Tunisia until May 1943.

WITH AFRICA FINALLY CLEARED OF GERMAN ARMIES, the Allies turned their attention across the Mediterranean. In July 1943 they invaded Sicily from the sea. Directed by General Dwight D. "Ike" Eisenhower and led by such charismatic generals as tank commander George C. Patton, Allied soldiers quickly rolled over the weak Italian forces.

PARIS, 1940

THE "BIG THREE": The depth of Hitler's threat may be judged by the unusual alliance of enemies he created. Franklin Roosevelt and Winston Churchill first met with unlikely bedfellow Joseph Stalin at Tehran late in 1943; the two promised Stalin they'd invade France in 1944

Polish forces stormed the Germans' seemingly impregnable stronghold at Monte Cassino and the forces at Anzio broke through the German line—that Hitler's grip over Italy was broken. Allied troops entered Rome on June 5, 1944, one day before the Allies finally opened the "second front."

THE DECISION TO LAUNCH A POTENTIALLY DECISIVE thrust at Hitler's western flank was confirmed in November 1943 at the first meeting of Stalin, Roosevelt and Churchill in Iran's capital, Tehran. While Soviet Russia was staving off the German dictator's armies at an exorbitant cost in lives in 1942 and 1943, Stalin had demanded that his allies open a front on the west, but Churchill and Roosevelt convinced him their armies weren't ready. Now the three men agreed: in 1944, Allied armies would invade occupied France and launch a major offensive to bring down Hitler's empire.

The grand strategy was now in place, but three links critical to its success remained to be fully forged: a plan of attack must be conceived, a leader strong enough to implement it must be found, and a vast force to carry it out must be assembled. The answers to those three questions would soon take shape, in the form of Operation Overlord, General Dwight D. Eisenhower and the Allied Expeditionary Force. The calendar toward D-day had begun to count down. ■

Soon dictator Benito Mussolini was deposed—and Italy's de facto new master became Adolf Hitler, who rushed German divisions into the peninsula. The Allied drive now bogged down; when British and U.S. forces launched a surprise seaborne invasion behind the German lines at the port of Anzio on Jan. 22, 1944, they suffered enormous losses and were bottled up for 123 days. The Germans fortified a strong defensive line across the midsection of Italy's "boot," just south of Rome. It was not until the late spring of 1944—after

WAR'S TOLL: The Allied assault on Italy bogged down at Monte Cassino, a 1,700-ft. peak that was home to a historic Benedictine monastery. After months of fighting reduced the monastery to rubble, the German grip was broken. Rome fell to the Allies one day before D-day

ITALY, 1944

MINES

SHAEF

Marching Orders

In size and complexity, Operation Overlord dwarfed all prior seaborne invasions. Allied planners had it all under control—except the weather

THE PREAMBLE TO "OUTLINE OF OPERATION OVERLORD," one of the classified briefing books prepared by the Supreme Headquarters Allied Expeditionary Force (SHAEF) in 1944, states that "an operation of the nature and size of Operation Overlord has never been previously attempted in history." And with good reason. Although in hindsight the logic of D-day may seem both obvious and inevitable, it appeared to be neither at the time. Generations of military planners had held amphibious landings in low regard, and the idea of staging one across the English Channel seemed particularly dubious. Napoleon had ached to cross the Channel and invade England, but he despaired of the obstacles. Adolf Hitler harbored the same ambition and reached the same conclusion. Both gambled on conquering Russia instead; both lost the wager.

Winston Churchill—his perspective steeped in the nine centuries of history since the last successful military assault across the Channel (the Norman Conquest, in 1066) and still smarting from the trauma of Dunkirk—had deep reservations about the idea. Instead, the British preferred to jab at the margins of Hitler's empire, invading North Africa and Italy while trying to bomb Germany into submission.

The Americans, however, were determined to assault the Nazis head-on. Spurred by the development of new technologies (like high-speed landing craft that could disgorge men and equipment on the beach itself) and the success of

THE PLAN: Under a compromise worked out by Churchill and Roosevelt, an American, Eisenhower, was the leader of Overlord, while his three key deputies were Britons

amphibious landings in the Pacific, U.S. war planners initially called for a small-scale invasion of northern France in late 1942, followed by a series of larger landings in 1943. Although logistical difficulties and tactical realities made these ideas nonstarters, the Western Allies promised Joseph Stalin in late 1943 that they would invade France the following spring.

Since the bulk of the forces would be American, General Dwight D. Eisenhower was chosen to lead the invasion, and the air, naval and ground forces were commanded by Englishmen: Air Chief Marshal Trafford Leigh-Mallory, Admiral Bertram Ramsey and General Bernard Montgomery. The British also christened the operation, Churchill selecting "Overlord" from a list of generic code names.

Eisenhower and his new staff inherited an invasion scheme that called for landing three divisions along a 35-mile front. That wasn't enough, said Montgomery. Ike agreed, calling for five divisions—150,000 men—to land along a front 50 miles wide. But Eisenhower overruled the British air commanders, who urged ongoing bombing of German oil refineries. Ike believed targeting supply lines—railroads and bridges—was more important, and his Transportation Plan was adopted.

The Germans knew that any sizable invading force would

Allied Invasions: Blueprints for Victory—and Calamity

DIEPPE, 1942

ANZIO, 1944

Overlord's planners learned from experience, basing their plans on Allied landings in France, Italy, Africa and the Pacific. A key lesson: the failed August 1942 invasion of Dieppe. More than two-thirds of the 6,000 gutsy Canadians who landed at this heavily fortified port city in eastern Normandy were killed, wounded or captured, proving that a frontal attack on a well-defended harbor was futile. The January 1944 landing at Anzio in Italy was flawed, but it finally succeeded. The lesson: attack lightly defended beaches and move men and supplies inland quickly.

be cut off from reinforcements and supplies unless a large harbor through which to funnel vast quantities of both could be captured early on. So the Nazis heavily fortified every major port in Western Europe. But German planners didn't anticipate that the Allies wouldn't need to capture a harbor if they could make one. The crucial innovation of using sunken ships and massive artificial breakwaters to build two temporary ports became a central element in Overlord. Once freed from targeting a port city, the landings could take place at a location of the Allies' choosing, one with comparatively light defenses, where the Germans wouldn't expect an attack. This aspect—surprise—was Overlord's second major feature. As the "Outline" put it, "Every effort must be made to draw the enemy's attention to our most favorable landing place, Pas de Calais, and away from our actual landing point, the Caen area."

The most daunting ingredient of Overlord, though, was its size and complexity. The critical component—an amphibious landing—called for massive, synchronized support: from

bombers, fighters, gliders and paratroopers in the air; from battleships, destroyers, midget subs, transports and landing ships on the sea; from scientists, engineers, medics, nurses and quartermasters on the ground. The numbers were staggering: some 5,000 ships would help land 150,000 men, as some 19,000 paratroopers and glider-borne infantry surprised the Germans behind the lines, all supported by thousands of bombing runs and hours of naval bombardment.

However complicated the operation, at least it could be planned. But the most critical element—the weather—didn't report to Ike. The invaders required clear skies for air support to be effective, moonlight for visibility and reasonably calm seas to approach the beaches. Tides were crucial: planners needed a day when the tides would be low just as the sun rose so that the first wave of landing craft could ride around obstacles that would later be submerged, then could float over them and back into the Channel as the water rose. The Germans, using past Allied invasions as guides, believed the Allies would only attack at high tide. It was a crucial error. ∎

The English Channel: Britain's Moat

The Romans and Vikings proved that England was vulnerable to attack from the sea; the Norman Conquest in 1066 was a sort of D-day in reverse. Napoleon's grand plan, at right, envisioned a multifaceted cross-Channel attack: from the air (using giant hot air balloons to ferry thousands of troops); from the sea (via "floating forts" that would stretch from Calais to Dover); from under the sea (he discussed designs for submarines with steamboat pioneer Robert Fulton); and even from under the ground, via tunnel. Although air support, pontoon bridges and submarine warfare would all eventually play a role in a successful military Channel crossing, they would have to wait more than a century, for Overlord.

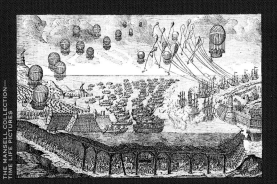

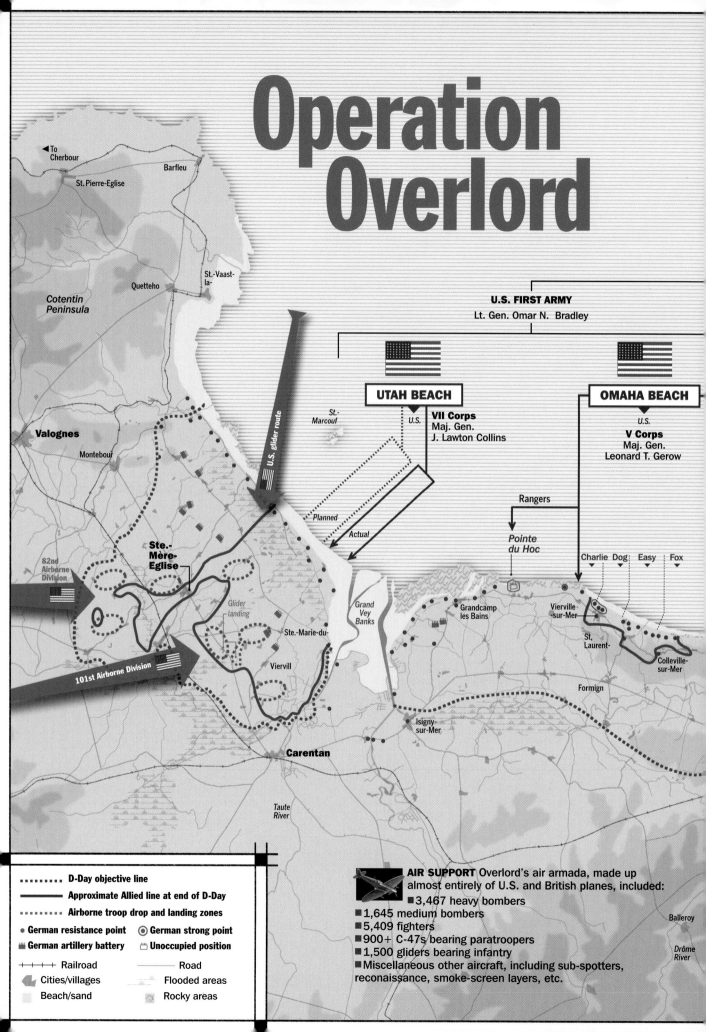

Operation Overlord

◄To Cherbour

Barfleu

St. Pierre-Eglise

St.-Vaast-la-

Quetteho

Cotentin Peninsula

Valognes

Montebour

St.-Marcouf

U.S. FIRST ARMY
Lt. Gen. Omar N. Bradley

UTAH BEACH

U.S.

VII Corps
Maj. Gen.
J. Lawton Collins

OMAHA BEACH

U.S.

V Corps
Maj. Gen.
Leonard T. Gerow

Rangers

Pointe du Hoc

Charlie Dog Easy Fox

U.S. glider route

Planned

Actual

Ste.-Mère-Eglise

82nd Airborne Division

Glider landing

Ste.-Marie-du-

Viervill

Grand Vey Banks

Grandcamp les Bains

Vierville-sur-Mer

St, Laurent-

Colleville-sur-Mer

Formign

101st Airborne Division

Isigny-sur-Mer

Carentan

Taute River

Balleroy

Drôme River

Legend

- **.........** D-Day objective line
- **———** Approximate Allied line at end of D-Day
- **- - - - - -** Airborne troop drop and landing zones
- • German resistance point
- ◉ German strong point
- ▥ German artillery battery
- ⌂ Unoccupied position
- +++++ Railroad
- ——— Road
- Cities/villages
- Flooded areas
- Beach/sand
- Rocky areas

AIR SUPPORT Overlord's air armada, made up almost entirely of U.S. and British planes, included:
- ■ 3,467 heavy bombers
- ■ 1,645 medium bombers
- ■ 5,409 fighters
- ■ 900+ C-47s bearing paratroopers
- ■ 1,500 gliders bearing infantry
- ■ Miscellaneous other aircraft, including sub-spotters, reconaissance, smoke-screen layers, etc.

The greatest invasion in history relied on an intricate multi-part attack. A prolonged aerial bombardment in the weeks leading up to D-day was followed by further air attacks on German positions in the early hours of June 6. Beginning around 0500 hours, Navy guns again hammered the Germans; the amphibious landings followed. In addition, some 24,000 men made airborne landings in Normandy, either by parachuting or landing in gliders.

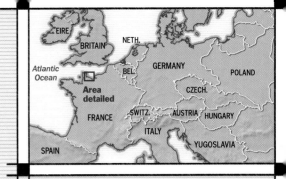

21st ARMY GROUP
Gen. Bernard L. Montgomery

BRITISH SECOND ARMY
Lt. Gen. Miles C. Dempsey

GOLD BEACH	**JUNO BEACH**	**SWORD BEACH**
British	*Canadian*	*British*
XXX Corps Lt. Gen. Gerard Bucknall	**I Corps** Lt. Gen. John T. Crocker	

Bay of the Seine

British 6th Airborne Division (gliders)

Item Jig King Love Mike Nan Oboe Peter Queen Roger

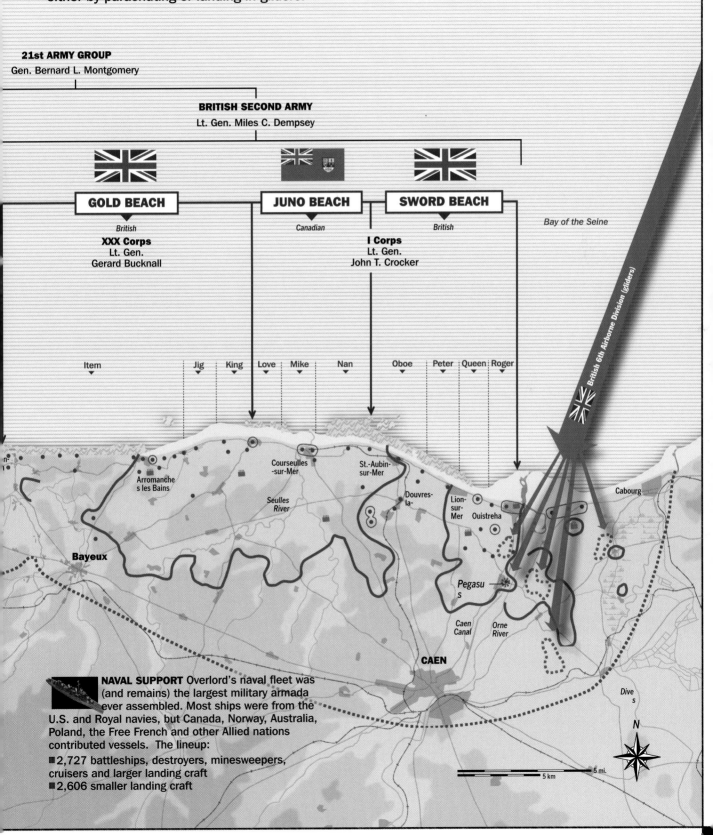

Arromanches les Bains
Courseulles-sur-Mer
St.-Aubin-sur-Mer
Douvres-la-
Seulles River
Cabourg
Lion-sur-Mer Ouistreha
Bayeux
Pegasus
Caen Canal Orne River
CAEN
Dives

N

NAVAL SUPPORT Overlord's naval fleet was (and remains) the largest military armada ever assembled. Most ships were from the U.S. and Royal navies, but Canada, Norway, Australia, Poland, the Free French and other Allied nations contributed vessels. The lineup:
- 2,727 battleships, destroyers, minesweepers, cruisers and larger landing craft
- 2,606 smaller landing craft

5 km   5 mi.

TOP BRASS: Ike, with Britain's Field Marshal Bernard Montgomery at his shoulder, gives Allied troops the once-over. The two commanders frequently clashed

"You will enter the continent of Europe and ... undertake operations aimed at the heart of Germany and the destruction of her armed forces."

— Eisenhower's orders

Ike's Invasion

The burden of Operation Overlord—the largest military undertaking in history—rested on the shoulders of a driven, demanding general

ONLY THE SUPREME COMMANDER COULD GIVE THE ORDER to attack. On the morning of June 5, screaming winds rattled the windows of the British naval headquarters near Portsmouth, where the D-day commanders were meeting and the rain, as General Dwight D. Eisenhower later recalled, lashed down in "horizontal streaks." Operation Overlord, slated to kick off that day, had already been delayed. Now Royal Air Force meteorologist J.N. Stagg cautiously predicted clearing skies for the next day. Eisenhower conferred with the generals and admirals gathered around him. He thought for less than a minute, then stood up. "O.K.," he said, "let's go."

From the idea to the word "go," Eisenhower had traveled a long, lonely road. Almost from the day America entered the war after the Japanese attacked Pearl Harbor in 1941, U.S. military leaders wanted to fight Hitler by invading through France. It would be risky, but if it succeeded, it would open the most di-

rect route across Europe into the heart of Germany. One of the earliest and most determined advocates for this approach was a young officer who had chosen a career in the military only after a knee injury had placed his first love, professional football, beyond reach. In March 1942, when Dwight David Eisenhower was chief of the War Department's Operations Division in Washington, he sent a memorandum on strategy to the austere, brilliant head of the U.S. Army, General George Marshall, urging that "the principal target for our first major offensive should be Germany, to be attacked through Western Europe." Eisenhower pointed out that in order to pull together the troops, training, transport and weapons for such a huge effort, the British and American governments would have to commit themselves formally to a cross-Channel attack.

President Franklin Roosevelt approved; in April 1942 he dispatched Marshall and presidential adviser Harry Hopkins to persuade Churchill in London. But the Allies had neither the troops nor the landing craft needed to carry out Operation Sledgehammer or Roundup or the other code-named plans to invade France in 1942 or 1943. Yet to boost national morale, both Churchill and Roosevelt were determined to mount an offensive somewhere against the Germans before 1942 ended. They decided to invade North Africa to drive out the Italians and the German Afrika Korps, though Marshall and Eisenhower opposed the move as a diversion of resources.

Eisenhower, now a lieutenant general based in London, was chosen to command Operation Torch, which went ashore in Morocco and Algeria in November 1942. His forces then moved into Tunisia to link up with Field Marshal Bernard Montgomery's Eighth Army, freeing all North Africa from the Axis. By 1943, when the Allies were ready to plan a Normandy attack, Eisenhower had commanded two more seaborne invasions: Sicily and mainland Italy. They were sideshows in his eyes—and the Italian campaign quickly bogged down into a bloody mile-by-mile struggle up the peninsula—but they taught him a great deal about the complexities of such operations. Equally important, he and Generals Omar Bradley and George Patton emerged from the North African and Italian battlefields as first-class combat leaders.

On a night of pea-soup fog in January 1944, Eisenhower arrived in London as Supreme Commander of the Allied Expeditionary Force that would invade the Continent. Roosevelt had decided he simply could not spare Chief of Staff Marshall, the man everyone assumed would command D-day. Instead the order signed by Britain and the U.S. went to Eisenhower: "You will enter the continent of Europe and, in conjunction with the other United Nations, undertake operations aimed at the heart of Germany and the destruction of her armed forces."

Americans who remember Ike at all tend to recall a do-little President or a mangler of sentences at press conferences. Military writers sometimes portray Ike the General as a genial and soothing Alliance board chairman at best, or at worst a gladhanding bumbler. Eisenhower the Supreme Commander was none of those. He was a driven, demanding man of terrific energy: up before dawn, to bed after midnight, chain-smoking four packs of cigarettes and drinking 15 cups of coffee a day. He was a military perfectionist, impatient with his subordinates and a peerless, lucid briefer. He had a volcanic temper he struggled to control but sometimes used as a tool. He was naturally friendly, with a famous grin, and he inspired trust. But he was patient only when he had to be: to keep peace among the Allies, since he believed the war would be won only if the Americans and British worked together.

Ike held the team together; it was perhaps his finest achievement. And now, after years of preparation, it had all come down to the words "Let's go." Once the order to launch Operation Overlord had been given, Eisenhower drove to nearby Newbury to say farewell to some of the 23,000 Allied paratroopers who would take off before midnight to drop behind the Germans' beach defenses. Eisenhower chatted with men of the U.S. 101st Airborne Division, wished them luck and shook hands with their commander, Brigadier General Maxwell Taylor. As their C-47 transports roared off toward France, the Supreme Commander stood with his staff on the roof of a headquarters building and saluted them. When he turned away, Eisenhower had tears in his eyes. ■

Artifact

Overlord's leader had to be an American, for the U.S. supplied most of its soldiers and weapons. Army Chief of Staff George Marshall longed to head the invasion, but Roosevelt couldn't part with him. When the two agreed on Eisenhower, Marshall saved the draft of the note F.D.R. sent to Stalin on the decision and passed it on to Ike

KEYSTONE VIEW

1916: With Mamie

A Life in Uniform

Dwight David Eisenhower was the third of six sons born to a Kansas creamery worker. After young Ike wasn't accepted to the Naval Academy, his first choice, he orchestrated a letter-writing campaign to clinch admission to West Point. His talent for organization

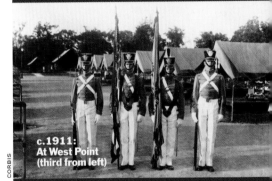

CORBIS

c.1911: At West Point (third from left)

made Eisenhower much coveted as a staff officer but kept him Stateside in World War I. In 1916 he married Mamie Geneva Doud, a millionaire meat-packer's daughter. Ike's career stalled at the rank of major for 16 years; it gathered steam after he served with General Douglas MacArthur in Washington, D.C., and the Philippines. In early 1942, Ike began helping Army Chief of Staff George Marshall plan war strategy, while lobbying hard to be sent to the front lines. Before the year was out, Marshall granted his protégé's wish, sending Ike to command the Allied invasion of North Africa.

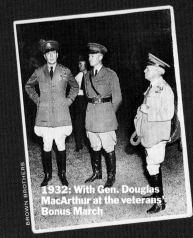

BROWN BROTHERS

1932: With Gen. Douglas MacArthur at the veterans' Bonus March

DEVON, APRIL 1944

GRANDSTAND SEAT: British schoolboys join an American guard as they watch Allied forces practicing invasion tactics. The place: Slapton Sands, where more than 700 soldiers would die within the month, when German boats attacked ships in Operation Tiger, a trial run for Overlord

> "An Anglo-American landing in the West will and must come. How and where it will come no one knows." — Adolf Hitler

The Buildup

Britain becomes an armed camp as a huge invasion force takes shape

S THE YEAR 1943 ENDED AND 1944 BEGAN, A SINGLE question dominated the thoughts of millions of people around the globe. From Adolf Hitler's mountain retreat in Berchtesgaden to the living rooms of Iowa farmers, from clandestine radios in Budapest to secret shortwave setups in the safe rooms of the French Resistance, men and women listened to the news and wondered, Was this the year when the long-anticipated "second front" would send Allied troops to invade Hitler's Fortress Europe? In a few highly secure rooms, there was no such uncertainty. In Joseph Stalin's office in the Kremlin, in the Map Room at the White House—

where Franklin Roosevelt followed the news from the fronts on oversized charts—and in Winston Churchill's underground bunker beneath London's streets, all was clear. At their first meeting, in Tehran in November, the "Big Three" Allied chieftains had agreed that the invasion would be launched on the French coast in the spring.

The man to lead it was in place: U.S. General Dwight D. Eisenhower, commander of Allied landings in North Africa, Sicily and Italy. A plan, now known as Operation Overlord, was well under way. The winter and early spring would be devoted to the most difficult aspect of the invasion—aggregating

FRANK SCHERSCHEL—TIME LIFE PICTURES

MARCH MARCH: U.S. troops hit the road in March in the U.K., as they toughen up for the invasion. The location was undisclosed, held back by military censors

buildup of men and supplies was taking place in Britain. In fact, under the original Overlord plan, D-day was planned for early in May, but when Montgomery took up his post as Eisenhower's deputy for ground forces in January, he immediately balked at the preliminary plans for a 25-mile-wide invasion front. He told Ike, who already had strong misgivings of his own, that the front must be much broader, about 50 miles, so that the Allies could land at least five divisions, instead of the planned three. The planners said they did not have enough landing craft for such an expansion. Get them, said Montgomery. That was impossible by the May deadline, said the planners. Then change the deadline, said Monty. They changed it.

Now, in Britain's streets, in the offices and pubs, the pace was quickening. "Strap-hanging across the Atlantic," a London newspaper called the steady flow of young soldiers into the small island. Uniforms of all nations thronged the streets of London and other major cities. A Glasgow police court, convicting a brothel keeper, described her house as "a miniature League of Nations." Tough, confident boys from Virginia, Kentucky and Montana chatted up the local girls; their Allied Expeditionary Force shoulder patches revealed they were just passing through.

British newspapers were filled with talk of Anglo-American understanding and friendship; Oxford and Cambridge opened their doors to American soldiers on furlough; Britons hosted "Hands Across the Water" parties, organized clubs and canteens, filled churches to overflowing. But there were tensions. The U.S. soldiers were better paid than the British troops; their uniforms were newer; and their accents and attitudes proved of great interest to the young British women at the pubs and parties. Before long, the state of affairs was summarized in a terse aphorism: the young Yanks, their British allies tut-tutted, were "overpaid, oversexed and over here."

the enormous forces needed to carry out the plan. The numbers were staggering: Overlord called for some 5,000 ships, more than 150,000 invasion troops, 19,000 paratroopers, thousands of bombers and gliders and fighters.

With information scarce, soldiers and civilians alike shared rumors and conjectures. When would the invasion be launched? Where would it strike? Most eyes turned to the coastal bulge known as the Pas de Calais, only 20 miles across the English Channel from Dover. In its first issue of 1944, TIME reported on a massive Allied bombing campaign there. "It might have been the herald of invasion," the magazine said. "It might have been practice for invasion. Or it might have been a calculated blow at some Nazi threat to coming invaders—or to England ..." The straining for clues was evident.

In that same issue, TIME reported on the choices of Eisenhower to lead the invasion and Britain's Field Marshal Bernard Montgomery as his second-in-command. The magazine went on to speculate about the timing of the attack, already using the military shorthand that would brand the date in the history books: "D-day was still the war's tightest secret. But this much is certain: it will be the earliest day on which 1) the problems of logistics and planning have been licked; 2) the all-important weather is friendly."

TIME's crystal ball wasn't all that powerful: an enormous

IMPERIAL WAR MUSEUM

DUMMY: This painted plywood "tank" may look all too fraudulent up close, but to prying German aviators, it will seem to be part of Britain's ersatz "Fourth Army"

ARSENAL: At top, P-51 Mustang fighters, with wingtips removed for travel, roll through an unidentified city. Below, women of the Auxiliary Territorial Service waterproof guns. Thousands of women served in this home-guard force. Their anthem boasted, "It's beauty on duty, grim and gay in the A.T.S."

Sadly, in one of the many ironies of World War II, the U.S. forces that came together to combat Hitler's racist regime reflected the segregation that prevailed in America at the time. Both the U.S. Army and Navy were divided into hierarchies: officers and key combat divisions were almost entirely white, while blacks filled rear-echelon and subordinate positions. Tens of thousands of black U.S. soldiers were in Britain in the spring of 1944; with black and white units bunking cheek by jowl, tensions flared. Again and again MPs had to break up fights between Americans in pubs. British women, many of whom had never encountered a black person before, offered a friendly welcome to America's African-American servicemen, to the annoyance of many white soldiers. Finally, Eisenhower ordered commanders to segregate troop leaves by race, with the result that Britain's pubs suddenly found themselves replicating the unfortunate "separate but equal" policies of America: they were jammed with black troops one night and white troops the next.

ACROSS THE CHANNEL, THE GERMANS KNEW AN INVASION WAS INEVITABLE. "AN Anglo-American landing in the West will and must come," Hitler told his key commanders that spring, but he added, "How and where it will come no one knows." The obvious choice: the Pas de Calais. That was where Field Marshal Erwin Rommel, whom Hitler had assigned to defend the Atlantic Wall, expected the landing. Rommel deployed his whole Fifteenth Army there, 208,000 men, to de-

Dress Rehearsals

Allied troops practiced over and over to mesh the complex gears of a sea-land invasion. The sequence of pictures below provides an overview of the trial runs. At top, U.S. troops practice moving trucks from a transport ship onto a "rhino" ferry. The last three pictures were shot on the coast of Scotland, showing Allied platoons storming off landing ships and clambering up a bluff. The last picture shows the mock invasion force unloading equipment onto a secure beachhead. The practice locations were carefully scouted to reflect the exact topography of the Normandy coast.

PAUSE THAT REFRESHES: British women—of all ages—offer coffee and charm to visiting American troops

supplies to the Allied front lines—in place of the French locomotives and cars that were being destroyed almost nightly by Allied bombers. And since the targeted beachfronts lacked harbors, a key reason the Germans didn't anticipate landings there, Allied engineers put the final touches on the enormous artificial harbors they would tow across the Channel and moor in place once the beaches were won.

The meadows, beaches and cliffs of the British Isles now became a surrogate France, as officers strained to prepare their recruits, most of whom had never seen combat, for the invasion. Bob Slaughter, an infantryman who trained at Tidworth, Scotland, recalled the experience in Gerald Astor's collection of oral histories, *June 6, 1944: The Voices of D-day:* "The instructors … were old-school, ruthlessly harsh, strict disciplinarians. Grueling speed marches, mountain and cliff climbing, unarmed combat, boat drills, exercise with logs, finding one's way on the desolate Scottish moors with nothing but a compass and map …" When a man dropped out, Slaughter recalled, the British instructor, who carried a foot-long leather swagger stick, flailed the young man's shoulders, calling him a "yellow-bellied coward unfit to breathe fresh air!"

On the night of April 27-28, the rehearsals proved all too real and all too deadly. As the U.S. VII Corps was practicing a seaborne invasion at Slapton Sands on the South Devon coast, German E-boats ("enemy boats," midsize cruisers that preyed on merchant convoys and smaller navy ships) penetrated a de-

fend every mile of beach. "The first 24 hours will be decisive," he said. He was right.

The Allies went to great lengths to nourish this German illusion. They repeatedly bombed and shelled the Calais area as though to soften it up for an invasion. They even created an illusory docking area near Dover, complete with phoney tanks, fake landing barges, dummy warehouses and barracks. Eisenhower assigned Lieut. General George S. Patton Jr.—who was in hot water for a notorious 1943 incident in which he slapped a shell-shocked soldier in Sicily—to command a phantom "First United States Army Group." TIME, LIFE and U.S. newsreels showed Patton strutting and fretting as he inspected troops from his supposedly massive army. It was a masterly piece of false intelligence, and the Germans fell for it. The British pitched in, creating an equally bogus "Fourth Army" in Edinburgh to threaten an invasion of Norway.

April—projected as a possible invasion month by TIME in January—came and went. No invasion. But the buildup accelerated, as all of southern England was transformed into an arsenal and point of departure. Allied engineers built 163 new airfields; pilots joked they could taxi the length of the island without touching grass. Allied quartermasters shipped in 2 million tons of weapons and supplies, 1,500 tanks, mountains of food and fuel. Allied work units built 170 new miles of railroad line to move the supplies into position. Down the gleaming new rails rolled 1,000 new locomotives and 20,000 new freight and tanker cars, ready to be ferried across the Channel after the invasion to move

Artifact

Evacuation Order

As early as December, British citizens were being rousted from their homes as Allied forces undertook practice maneuvers. The notice at left, issued to residents of the South Hams region—and posted just in time for Christmas—warns that electric power will be turned off on Dec. 21. Most Britons, TIME said, took such hardships in stride; after four years of being on the defensive, they were happy to see "our lads" preparing for an offensive thrust.

NOTICE.

The public are reminded that requisition took effect from November 16th, from which date compensation is calculated. They will *not*, except for special reason, be disturbed in their possession until December 21st, but from that date the Admiralty may at any time and without notice enforce their right to immediate possession. It is therefore essential that EVERY PERSON SHOULD LEAVE THE AREA BY DECEMBER 20th.

On December 21st the supply of electricity in the area will cease. The present measures for supplying food will not be continued, but will be replaced by arrangements of a purely emergency character. The police stations will be closing during the present week.

THE INFORMATI ENTRES will remain OPEN ... They will be CLOSE... ...ll be pr...

■■ countdown to d-day

fensive perimeter of Allied destroyers and opened fire: six landing ships were sunk and six others damaged. Some 750 men were killed and 300 wounded—a far higher total than would die on Utah Beach on D-day itself. The debacle only heightened the Allies' concerns.

As May drew to a close, the tension in headquarters mounted and preparations took on an air of last-minute urgency: the invasion was scheduled for Monday, June 5. The numbers involved were so massive that the landing divisions began loading onto their transport ships on May 31. There were 58,000 U.S. soldiers and 75,000 other troops, mainly British but also Canadian, Polish and Dutch. (One overage volunteer begged Eisenhower to be allowed to join a landing party, but Ike flatly rejected Winston Churchill's plea.)

By June 3 the loading was complete. But the weather turned against the Allies. Even as infantry troops began filing onto the ships and the vast naval armada began steaming into the Channel, a major storm—the worst in years—turned the skies turbulent and the waves choppy. At 0400 hours on Sunday, June 4, chief meteorologist J.M. Stagg told Ike and his staff that the weather was worsening. Dejected and upset, Ike overruled Montgomery, who wanted to proceed, and put off the invasion for one day. Off the coast, the convoy of ships

DO YOUR DUTY: The mightiest army in history may be assembling, but it's still laundry day for these locals

made a U-turn. Aboard them, tens of thousands of seasick men, tuned up for action, would have to wait another day.

The news was better early the next morning: Stagg predicted the front would lift, though he couldn't say for how long. Eisenhower gave the order to go, and the clock toward H-hour began ticking down. Soon, across southern Britain, airplane engines would be revving up, propellers would be turning and eyes would scan the skies, where the invasion of Fortress Europe would begin, led by the paratroopers. ■

HURRY UP—AND WAIT: Traffic jams were a common snafu as the huge force assembled. Pre-invasion jitters? Not here: most of these U.S. soldiers seem happy, though one is obviously at the end of his rope

HULTON ARCHIVE—GETTY IMAGES

The Paratroopers

SITUATION REPORT **Operation Neptune** A convoy of more than 200 minesweepers has departed Area Z, south of the Isle of Wight, and begun clearing a path across the channel for the invasion fleet • **Operation Coup de Main** British glider troops are on the ground at Bénouville, engaging the enemy at two bridges • **Landings** Final orders have been issued to ground troops who will assault Gold, Sword, Juno, Omaha, and Utah beaches. Troop transport ships are assembling at Area Z for Channel crossing

H-HOUR: Synchronize your watches! British pathfinder paratroopers are ready to take off on the evening of June 5. Hours later they would jump into Normandy, where, in general, the British chutists fared better than their U.S. colleagues

"One man dived out the door headfirst ... the next man made it crawling. Then I dived." —Sergeant Louis Truax

JUNE 5: Eisenhower visits the paratroopers of the 101st Airborne Division before they board their planes. He was warned that the men might sustain casualty rates as high as 75%; the final figure was much lower, closer to 10%

U.S. SIGNAL CORPS

A T THE STROKE OF MIDNIGHT, AS June 5 became June 6, Operation Overlord was already well off the ground—literally. Chugging toward the coast of occupied France was a vast convoy of airplanes, their bellies filled with paratroopers, for D-day would be fought not only on the beaches and cliffs of Normandy but also in its skies. The invasion began with the largest parachute drop yet attempted in warfare, a mind-boggling operation that saw more than one thousand Allied planes drop some 16,000 U.S. and 8,000 British paratroopers into the fields and hedgerows of Normandy, beyond the landing beaches on the coast. The Yanks' mission: secure Overlord's flank on the west. The Brits' goal: to seize and control the eastern flank.

These gutsy troops were the invasion's knife-point, and they would sustain serious losses on D-day and in the first few days that followed. In the last week before the men took to the skies, Eisenhower's British deputy for air operations, Air Chief Marshal Trafford Leigh-Mallory, formally protested to Ike about the planned U.S. parachute assault, which he said would result in the "futile slaughter of two fine divi-

GEARING UP: U.S. paratroopers move to their Douglas C-47s on June 5

sions." Ike weighed the objection and decided to go on. Some slaughter did follow; so did victory.

Viewed in detail, as a series of individual events, the parachute operation was in some ways a disaster, a series of miscues and snafus that suggest a complete failure. But despite all the misadventures that accompanied the drop, the presence of thousands of Allied soldiers within and behind their lines utterly confused the Germans, who had no clear idea of just how many paratroopers had dropped, much less in what locations. Thus, though Allied pilots in many cases failed to deliver the troopers to their targets and many individual objectives were not reached, the drop helped stymie the German response. Overall, most historians now agree, paratroopers played a critical role in the success of the invasion.

A TIME writer watched the takeoff and caught the tension of the scene: "Inside a barbed-wire enclosure, where the crews of a troop carrier squadron were confined like some kind of rare and precious birds, a whistle skirled. Pilots, co-pilots, navigators turned out, listened to the briefing. They squinted at the sky. It was a squally night with a fitful, pale moon. The men climbed into trucks, whipped off to the airfield. Already a clattering rumble spread across

A paratrooper packs his flight bag

One Man's Drop

Ralph K. Manley, 20, jumped into Normandy outside Carenton in the early hours of June 6, as a private in the 101st Airborne Division. He recalled that experience for this book.

As Manley waddled onto his C-47 in England on June 5, he stepped on a scale to record his weight: 417 lbs. He carried:
- 50 lbs. of 2.5-lb. explosives in two 25-lb. bags fastened to his legs
- Fuses, primer cord, blasting caps and a detonator for the explosives
- Three 10-lb. antitank mines
- An 85-lb. flamethrower and gelatinized gasoline
- A folding-stock carbine weapon and 100 rounds of ammunition
- Six hand grenades, a .45-cal. pistol and 50 rounds of ammunition
- Three knives: one on his leg, one in his collar, a smaller one on his ankle
- A cricket clicker for identification
- Main parachute on his back, reserve parachute on his front
- Three boxes of K rations
- Rope, shovel, helmet, flashlight, field glasses, canteen of water, Halizone pills to purify water, "Mae West" life preserver
- Musette bag with socks, personal items, three condoms (useful for keeping mud and sand out of rifle barrels)
- French francs printed in America (about $25 worth)
- First-aid packets, including one containing morphine

When his unit began its drop, the plane was hit; it caught fire and started going down. Manley was the third man to jump from the burning craft. Two more followed, but the sixth soldier was hit in the doorway, blocking the other troopers; all 13 died when the plane crashed.

Manley survived the war; his twin brother died in Africa. Now a vigorous 80 years old and a city councilman in Springfield, Mo., Manley plans to return to Normandy for an anniversary jump in June 2004.

Artifact

The "Cricket" Clicker

One of the more unusual—and more inexpensive—weapons in the fascinating arsenal of D-day was a child's toy: a small, simple metal "cricket" that made a one-two snapping sound. All paratroopers were issued these, and they worked effectively to help soldiers locate each other in the dark. Once initial contact had been made, the password for recognition on D-day night was the call-and-response "Thunder … lightning."

THE DROP: The large bag on the first trooper's chest is his extra chute. The harnesses of British chutes were superior to U.S. models; they were easier to slip out of. Many U.S. soldiers drowned in shallow water, dragged under by their sopping-wet chutes and unable to escape

the night-hung countryside: engines on the warmup. They piled out of trucks at the darkened stations and went to work.

"Paratroops, grotesque and awkward in their equipment, climbed into the C-47 transport planes [modified DC-3s]. In swift succession, the aircraft took off and crawled up toward the cloudy sky. With formation lights on because of the dense traffic, a parade of transports, gliders, tow planes, which in single file would have stretched more than 200 miles, droned across the English Channel. In the carriers, the paratroops dozed, or pretended to. They were the Army's élite, the tough boys—lean, wiry men clad in green camouflaged battled dress, faces stained with cocoa and linseed oil. ('We'll have something to eat if our rations run out.') They carried the fanciest arms, and the most primitive.

"Near midnight the first planes reached their objective near Cherbourg. Men snapped their rip cords over static lines, waited, crouching. The command came, and they leaped. White, yellow and red parachutes blossomed in the night. Men by the thousands, weapons by the thousands, floated down upon captive France."

THE PARATROOPERS OF D-DAY WERE PIONEERS OF A NEW kind of warfare. Just as the use of submarines and airplanes took combat into entire new realms in World War I, the notion of dropping infantrymen into battle from aircraft was a startling innovation in military strategy, first prac-

ticed by the Soviet Red Army in the 1930s. In *Six Armies in Normandy*, the eminent historian of warfare John Keegan describes a 1936 propaganda film that showed early Russian paratroopers: "Shot through the turbulence of the camera aircraft's slipstream, it had shown a file of wind-tortured automata climbing from the door of a giant Tupolev transport, clinging desperately to the rail along its fuselage as they breasted the chord of its monstrous wing and then, at a signal, releasing their grip in unison to be whirled away into invisibility …" The Germans proved the value of airborne infantry in 1941, using paratroopers to take over the island of Crete. When the U.S. entered the war, its two new paratroop units, the 82nd and 101st Airborne divisions, played important roles in the invasions of Tunisia and Sicily.

But Overlord's use of paratroopers was on a scale never dreamed of before: it took 822 C-47s, each carrying a "stick" of 18 men, to ferry the 16,000 U.S. paratroopers across the Channel. The C-47s flew in tight, nine-plane V formations across the choppy seas, an armada of shadows, only their lavender wing lights clearly visible in the moonlight. They took more than three hours to cross the strait, then dropped to 700 ft. to make their landing run. Suddenly they plunged into the turbulence of a thick bank of clouds. The pilots reflexively separated to avoid collision. As they emerged from the blinding clouds, sheets of flak began exploding all around them. Sergeant Louis Truax saw his plane's left wing hit, and then the paratroopers went sprawling. "One man dived out the door headfirst," he said. "I grabbed the ammo belt ... of the man I thought next and gave him a heave out nose first. The next man made it crawling ... Then I dived."

Many men were dropped miles from their landing sites, some were dropped far out at sea, some were dropped so low that their parachutes never opened. Private Donald Burgett recalled that the falling bodies "made a sound like large, ripe pumpkins being thrown down against the ground."

There was another unforeseen hazard. The crafty General Erwin Rommel

had dammed a number of rivers to flood the nearby fields, and many paratroopers landed with their burden of supplies in three or four feet of water. Private John Steele, whose story would be immortalized in Cornelius Ryan's *The Longest Day*, had a different kind of problem: his parachute caught on the steeple of the church in Ste.-Mère-Eglise, so he played dead while German patrols prowled the streets below. A stray bullet hit him in the foot. He watched another ammunition-laden paratrooper land directly on a burning house and explode. Others were shot while hanging in trees. After two hours, a German finally spotted Steele, cut him down and took him prisoner. American forces later rescued him when they occupied the town, the first in France to be liberated.

All night long the scattered paratroopers worked to re-gain contact, snapping their cricket noisemakers to locate each other. (Most of their radios had been lost, along with 60% of their other supplies). Sometimes the cricket sound drew German gunfire, but more often it brought lonely stragglers together into makeshift units. Others remained lost for days but worked independently to harass and confuse the enemy.

To the east, the British 6th Airborne had a somewhat easier time of it. In contrast to the Americans, most British pilots managed to land their "sticks" close to their targets just after midnight, catching the Germans by surprise. By dawn the troopers—in many cases working in collaboration with troops who landed by glider—had captured their two main objectives, the important bridges across the Orne and Dives rivers, securing the eastern flank of the British beach landing sites. It was a brilliant success.

The kick-off action of Operation Overlord didn't work like a charm—but it had worked. The attack on Fortress Europe had begun. ∎

CORBIS

Of Leaders and Legends

Two hallowed units of the U.S. Army forged links in their legends on June 6, 1944, and each was led by a commander who achieved further glory. Major General Maxwell Taylor, looking extra jaunty in the picture above, was the leader of the 101st Airborne Division; D-day was his fifth jump, qualifying him for his wings. He landed safely and began to use his cricket. "The first man I met in the darkness I thought was a German until he cricketed," he recalled. "He was the most beautiful soldier I'd ever seen, before or since. We threw our arms around each other, and from that moment I knew we had won the war." Taylor went on to serve his country with distinction in Korea, as Chairman of the Joint Chiefs of Staff and finally as ambassador to South Vietnam.

Commanding the U.S. 82nd Airborne Division was Major General Matthew Ridgway, a far more hard-nosed customer than the diplomatic Taylor. TIME depicted him as "a soldier who possesses a passionate sense of detail, an instinct for the bonds that unite a commander and his troops, and a nice flair for showmanship." Indeed. After he jumped into Normandy, Ridgway and an aide were surprised by a German tank. The aide dived into a hole, but Ridgway whipped his rifle to his shoulder and fired. For some inexplicable reason, the tank turned and clanked away. "I got him!" bellowed the exuberant boss of the 82nd.

Ridgway went on to command the Allied forces in Korea; with his signature hand grenade pinned to his chest, he is credited with restoring morale and purpose to an Army that had been badly mauled by Chinese troops. He later replaced Eisenhower as Supreme Allied Commander of NATO forces in Europe, then served as Army Chief of Staff.

COURTESY THE NATIONAL D-DAY MUSEUM (2)

Artifact

Dummy Paratrooper

Allied paratroopers who dropped into Normandy on D-day had a little help from an unusual friend: a dummy paratrooper, created to confuse and bewilder the Germans. "Rupert," at right, and his mates were cooked up by a British intelligence officer, Captain Michael R.D. Foot. The dummies were designed to self-destruct on landing, creating a minor explosion that would lead the Germans to believe there were far more troopers in the air than were actually there. The devices—like the dummy tanks and barracks dotting U.K. meadows—succeeded in baffling the enemy.

0100-0200 Hours

The Gliders

SITUATION REPORT **Operation Neptune** Naval assault forces are assembling off the Isle of Wight • **Airborne operations** First paratroopers have landed east of the Orne River and engaged German defenders. Additional transport planes are preparing to take off in southern England with second air wave • **The enemy** German communications report first sightings of paratroopers on ground

I**N THE SKIES ABOVE NORMANDY, ABOARD SHIPS IN THE** Channel, in communications rooms in southern England, radio operators sat hunched over their wireless sets, straining to pluck from the static the first tidings of victory or defeat in the great crusade that had begun just an hour earlier. It was shortly after 1 a.m. that three cryptic words crackled through all these headsets: "Ham and Jam … Ham and Jam … Ham and Jam …"

To those who knew what it meant, the urgently repeated phrase brought relief and a new determination to forge ahead with the next steps of Operation Overlord. "Ham and Jam" was the code to indicate that glider troops from the British 6th Airborne Division had stormed two bridges in the town of Bénouville—one over the Orne River and one crossing the Caen Canal—and taken them intact. Much of the success of D-day depended on taking and holding these bridges. In German hands, the crossings could be used to bring panzer tank units up from the rear to counterattack the British paratroop-

ers who would soon be landing behind Sword Beach. Conversely, if the Germans believed they were about to lose control of these important bridges, they might blow them up—thus slowing down the Allied breakout from Sword and impeding supply and reinforcement.

Regular parachute infantry had little chance of accomplishing Operation Coup de Main, as the mission for the two bridges was called, because the noise of their plane engines usually alerted enemy troops, while their slow, visible descent gave defenders on the ground plenty of warning, and they often landed far from their targets—and one another. Because speed, silence and surprise were vital, the only way to place the 181 troops under the command of Major John Howard on the ground and together, close to the target bridges, was to use silent glider planes.

Howard and his men had taken off from the Tarrant Rushton R.A.F. base in Dorset shortly after 11 p.m. the previous evening. At seven minutes after midnight, the convoy of six

> "Six thousand feet, six miles to go. The coast of France below and an uncanny silence."
>
> — Sergeant James Wallwork, glider pilot

Horsa gliders had been released from their Halifax bomber "tugs" just as they crossed the Normandy coast, marking the official beginning of D-day. Less than ten minutes later, they were on the ground at the bridges. In an assault that took not quite an hour, they stormed both spans, killing or wounding all of the surprised defenders before the Germans could put up more than token resistance or blow up either bridge. In the course of this action, two British glider troopers were killed—one of them, platoon commander Lieut. Denholm Brotheridge, was cut down while leading the charge across the Orne River Bridge, making him the first casualty of D-day. By

PRACTICE RUN: New British Hamilcar gliders are towed by Handley aircraft. On D-day, the British used Horsa gliders, 67 ft. long, with an 88-ft. wingspan, made of plywood and holding 30 men. The U.S. CG-4A gliders were 48 ft. long with an 84-ft. wingspan; made of plywood, canvas and steel tubing, they held 15 men

WORKHORSES: British troops of the 6th Airborne Division unload a jeep and and other equipment from a glider in Normandy. Far cheaper than airplanes—yet almost defenseless—the gliders were invaluable to quartermasters but could be deadly as infantry carriers

a few minutes past 1 a.m., Howard's radioman was reporting back that the bridges were secure.

The 6th Airborne Division team was one small part of the vast D-day glider airlift, which included 1,200 U.S. CG-4A gliders and 300 British Horsas. The glider-borne troops were given some of Overlord's most challenging and indispensable missions. They included assaults on strategic targets like the Bénouville bridges; tactical objectives like the fortified gun emplacement at Merville; and such difficult, dangerous tasks as ferrying behind enemy lines equipment too heavy to be dropped by parachute, such as jeeps, bulldozers and 75-mm howitzers. In most cases, glider troops acted as the tip of a spear that would be followed by an ever widening blade of regular paratroopers and ground infantry.

Sadly, glider troops were (and remain) among the least recognized of D-day's heroes, neglected perhaps because they were bureaucratic orphans: infantry commanders thought of glider troops as part of the Army Air Force, while Air Force leadership considered them infantrymen who happened to deploy from the air, somewhat like paratroopers.

This uncertain status, coupled with the high level of danger inherent in glider operations (more than one-third of all glider troops would be killed or wounded during the war), meant that many glider troops had little affection for their specialty. They derisively referred to their aircraft as "flying coffins," which was disturbingly close to the truth. When America entered the war, the Army discovered that there were no companies in the U.S. with experience in the mass-production of gliders. So it gave the supply contracts to firms that manufactured heavy wooden products but often had little knowledge of aeronautical engineering—among them casket makers, ice box factories and the Steinway piano company. The result was that U.S. Army gliders, especially in the early days of the war, would frequently break apart in mid-air or crash shortly after takeoff.

The irony was that the American and British armies were struggling to duplicate a program that the Germans had already abandoned as impractical and too costly. The glider race began in May 1940, when a team of 78 German troops landed silently on the roof of the Belgian fortress of Eben Emael, which was widely regarded as impregnable. Exploiting the advantage of surprise, they dropped explosives into the ventilation system and panicked the 850-man garrison, which quickly surrendered. A year later, the Allies were stunned when the Germans used gliders to land 13,000 paratroopers in broad daylight on the island of Crete, seizing it from the British. What neither the British nor the Americans knew, however, was that the Germans had lost 5,000 men in the assault on Crete, leading Hitler to conclude that glider operations exacted too high a cost in lives and matériel to justi-fy the gains they brought. He didn't use them again.

For Allied glider troops taking part in D-day, however, the danger in the air was only slightly less frightening than what awaited them on the ground. General Erwin Rommel had peppered the Normandy landscape with anti-glider obstacles that Allied troops would nickname "Rommel's asparagus"—12-ft.-tall poles, spaced 15 to 40 ft. apart and connected by trip wires to mines planted at their bases. These devices could shred an incoming glider, impale the men inside and tear apart with shrapnel anyone who survived. The Germans also flooded many of the fields that would lend themselves to glid-er landings, which meant that the aircraft (laden with men and equipment) would sink within seconds of touching down, drowning everyone inside.

Deadlier than the man-made obstacles, however, were those provided by nature. Allied reconnaissance had spotted Normandy's proliferation of hedgerows but inexplicably failed to notice their height. D-day planners had assumed they were English-style hedgerows, low enough for horse-back riders to jump. What glider pilots discovered instead were solid walls of foliage five to eight feet tall. Attempting to land, a pilot who approached a field high enough to clear one hedgerow would smash into the second before he could touch down and stop. If he attempted to pull up and clear the sec-ond hedgerow, the glider would stall and crash. (The hedgerows would not only disrupt the glider landings; the natural barriers would seriously delay the coming Allied thrust once the troops were off the beachheads.)

These dangers would claim dozens of lives on June 6, in-cluding that of the U.S. 101st Airborne's Brigadier General Donald F. Pratt, the most senior Allied casualty on D-day. They would also wreak havoc when more than half of the glid-ers used by the 82nd and 101st Airborne divisions missed their drop zones, as pilots who had never been exposed to anti-aircraft fire took excessive evasive measures, leaving troops who were supposed to link up with the beach landing forces by day's end both lost and bereft of heavy equipment.

But for all their imperfections, gliders were one of the keys to D-day's success, and Allied commanders continued to use them in almost every major action through the end of the war in Europe: the Battle of the Bulge, the liberation of Holland and the crossing of the Rhine into Germany. And even if his-tory has overlooked the men who descended from the sky in silence, the people of Bénouville have not. After the war, the two bridges captured in the early-morning hours of June 6 by John Howard and his men were given new names: Pegasus (in honor of the flying horse that graces the unit insignia of the Sixth Airborne Division) and Horsa (in honor of the gliders in which they landed). ∎

HEAVY TOLL: In a grim scene that was played out all too often on D-day, eight U.S. paratroopers lie dead near the wreckage of their glider outside Hiesville, France. Such images were not seen in America at the time; censors withheld photos of U.S. casualties until 1945

The Germans

SITUATION REPORT **Airborne Operations** The first waves of paratroopers and glider troops from the U.S. 82nd and 101st Airborne Divisions have landed behind the U.S. invasion beaches and are attempting to regroup. ● **Operation Neptune** U.S. and British minesweepers are crossing the Channel, clearing a path to the invasion beaches for the troopships ● **Aerial Bombardment** Heavy bombing raids against German coastal positions are in progress

"Our only possible chance [of stopping the Allies] will be at the beaches." —General Erwin Rommel

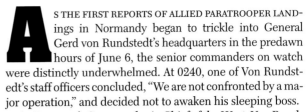

NORMANDY, SPRING, 1944

AS THE FIRST REPORTS OF ALLIED PARATROOPER LAND-ings in Normandy began to trickle into General Gerd von Rundstedt's headquarters in the predawn hours of June 6, the senior commanders on watch were distinctly underwhelmed. At 0240, one of Von Rundst-edt's staff officers concluded, "We are not confronted by a ma-jor operation," and decided not to awaken his sleeping boss.

As Germany's Commander in Chief of the West, Von Rund-stedt theoretically held dominion over an area that stretched from Norway to Spain, supervising 60 divisions of German troops. In reality, as Von Rundstedt himself observed in the spring of 1944, he had direct authority over the sentries on guard in front of his headquarters in St.-Germain-en-Laye, outside Paris, and not much else. An aristocratic Prussian gen-eral of the old school, Von Rundstedt scorned Adolf Hitler and resented the Austrian-born dictator's usurpation of his gener-als' powers. (In 1941, he had resigned from the army in protest when Hitler forbade a tactical withdrawal in Russia that Von Rundstedt advocated.) Hitler returned Von Rundstedt's scorn and assigned him to the largely honorary post of *Oberbe-felshaber* of the western front, in part to marginalize him.

The divisions over which Von Rundstedt had nominal com-mand were themselves marginal. By June 1944, the Third Reich's best troops were tied up in combat, either in Russia or Italy. The quiet duty of defending Western Europe fell to the very old and very young, to non-German troops who had vol-unteered in order to be released from POW camps, and to units made up of medically unfit personnel who had been mustered out of the front lines elsewhere.

But Von Rundstedt was too professional a soldier and too fervent a patriot to languish idly in France, presiding over skeletal units and scant fortifications. Instead, he drafted a re-port early in 1943 describing the woefully inadequate state of German defenses in Western Europe. Hitler responded by appointing Erwin Rommel, the young, ambitious "Desert Fox" of Africa, to oversee a new buildup of defenses in West-ern Europe. Although technically Von Rundstedt's subordi-nate, Rommel reported directly to Berlin and Hitler.

The dictator loved massive construction projects, concrete emblems of his power. By the end of 1942, 250,000 laborers were pouring 800,000 tons of concrete each month into the Atlantic Wall, the defensive shield for Fortress Europe. The re-sulting chain of more than 15,000 fortifications stretched along the shores of the North Sea, the English Channel, the Atlantic Ocean and France's Mediterranean coast. Its three ba-sic defensive structures included fortresses concentrated around major harbors, coastal batteries placed between har-bors to fire on Allied ships and *Widerstandnesten* ("resistance nests") positioned to repel landing troops on beaches.

The harbor fortresses, such as those at Cherbourg and Le Havre, held several dozen large-caliber guns (155 to 240 mm); these made France's port cities unassailable. The coastal batteries were equipped with medium-caliber guns (100 to 155 mm). The smaller, more lightly fortified *Wider-*

THE ATLANTIC WALL: General Erwin Rommel inspects German fortifications in Normandy. The "Desert Fox" and his titular superior, General Gerd von Rundstedt, clashed over the details of Hitler's defensive strategy

standnesten were built into cliffs, dunes and sea walls and contained smaller-caliber guns (50 to 88 mm). Positioned to rake the beaches with overlapping fields of fire, each "nest" included at least two pillboxes, plus open positions for mortar, machine-gun and antiaircraft pieces. These could be densely packed: at Omaha Beach there were scores of them.

Rommel believed mines were the best way to plug the numerous gaps he detected in the stone and steel of the Atlantic Wall. He oversaw the planting of more than 4 million of them: contact, antenna and pressure mines to blow up Allied ships as they approached the shore; Teller mines to wreck tanks and vehicles on the shore; and S-types (also known as "Bouncing Betties," because they popped up to waist height before detonating) to kill Allied infantry as they moved inland.

Rommel also devised numerous traps and obstacles to prevent Allied invaders from reaching the beach or slow them down once they arrived there. Among the devices he called "my inventions" were "Czech hedgehogs" (three 6-ft.-long pieces of railroad steel crossed and welded together in the center, set in a concrete base on the beach, to impale incoming landing craft); "Belgian gates" (submerged 7-by-10-ft. steel frames festooned with waterproof mines); "dragon's teeth" (rows of triangular concrete blocks, about 3 ft. high, to halt advancing tanks); and "tetrahedra" (concrete-and-steel pyramids to stop landing barges). Inland, Rommel prepared a welcome for airborne invaders. He planted "asparagus," heavy wooden stakes, into fields to shred glider bottoms. And he flooded lowland areas, hoping that heavily laden paratroopers might drown in even shallow water. He got his wish.

An impressive array—but chronic matériel shortages partially subverted this strategy of low-tech harassment. By the spring of 1944, less than 10% of the 50 million mines Rommel wanted to lay along the Atlantic Coast were in place. Of the thousands of bunkers facing the Channel, fewer than 1 in 6 was reinforced against heavy bombardment. And the larger artillery pieces were diverted almost exclusively to Russia. The Atlantic Wall came closest to matching its propaganda around major ports—especially in Pas de Calais, where Hitler imagined the invasion was coming. Rommel and Von Rundstedt agreed

Artifact

Goliath Remote-Controlled Tank

Easily among the odder armaments of World War II is this German mini-tank. About six ft. long and 3 ft. high, it resembles an overgrown toy—but it was packed with explosives. A few radio-controlled Goliaths were at Utah Beach on D-day, but the radio system went down, and they were not a factor.

that tank units would determine the outcome of the invasion. But Rommel wanted to use the tank units at the shore, to decimate the invaders at the moment of their greatest vulnerability. Von Rundstedt countered that keeping the tanks in reserve, far from the beaches, would allow the Germans to move them up and meet the Allies at the time and place of the Germans' choosing. In fact, the argument was entirely theoretical, for one man—Hitler—reserved control of the tank units in the West to himself, and he was thousands of miles from the battlefield.

It was this dilemma that Rommel hoped to resolve as he departed France for a short leave in Germany on June 4. He planned to visit with his wife at their country home in Ulm (he left toting a birthday present for her, a pair of custom-made shoes from a fashionable Paris boutique). Then he would make his case to Hitler personally at the Führer's retreat in Berchtesgaden. Rommel felt comfortable leaving the coast because he believed the Allies would not attack for some two weeks, when the high tides coincided with dawn, their strategy in prior invasions. But Operation Overlord's planners outfoxed the Desert Fox: they landed on a rising tide.

W HEN THE FIRST, FRAGMENTARY REPORTS OF PARATROOPER LANDINGS AND Allied ships in the Channel began to filter up two separate German chains of command in the early hours of June 6, no one had a sufficiently complete picture of events to believe that this was much more than a small-scale raid. Deception by Allied intelligence and sabotage of German communication lines by the French Resistance further addled the Germans, wasting precious hours. Even after it became apparent that a major invasion (if not *the* major invasion) was underway, local officers could do nothing: the power to command was in Hitler's hands. The day was almost over before he permitted his officers to respond to the invasion.

Rommel never made it to his meeting with Hitler. His staff, finally realizing that a major crisis was unfolding, reached him at home around 1000 on June 6, and Rommel decided to return to France immediately. Because the Allies had uncontested control of the skies, however, he didn't dare fly. By car, the trip took Rommel almost a full day; he didn't reach his headquarters in France until close to midnight. The day that was lost as Rommel sat in his car, fuming, was all the Allies needed.

The tale of Germany's Occupation of France is bracketed by two failed defensive lines. Hitler conquered the French in 1940 by rolling around their vaunted Maginot Line, proving it was useless. Four years later, the Allies began the liberation of the French by attacking Hitler's vaunted Atlantic Wall head-on, proving it was hollow. That wall, the product of four years of labor, held up the invaders for less than an hour at Utah Beach; about one hour at Sword, Juno and Gold beaches; and less than a day at Omaha Beach. And once the wall was down, all Hitler's forces and all Hitler's men couldn't put Fortress Europe together again. ■

SPRING CLEANING: German newspapers carried pictures of troops cleaning out their bunkers in Normandy after a harsh winter

Loyal to the End—Almost

H e was a master tactician who liked to attack from the east in the morning and the west in the afternoon, so the sun would always be in his enemy's eyes. But he was a mediocre strategist, gripped by manic highs when a battle was going his way and utter dejection when the tide turned. He was a glory-hound who staged re-enactments of his own victories for Nazi propaganda filmmakers (with his men dressed up as hapless British troops), but he was also an incorruptible patriot who declined Hitler's offer of a manorial farm as a reward for his deeds in Africa. He was a decent man who never joined the Nazi Party but a moral and political simpleton who idolized Hitler as Germany's savior until long after the truth should have been apparent. In short, Erwin Rommel was the sum of his contradictions.

Unlike the Prussian aristocrats who dominated Germany's officer corps, Rommel was born the son of a Swabian schoolmaster in 1891. He served with distinction in World War I and led Hitler's military bodyguard in the 1930s. In North Africa, his genius for battlefield improvisation and daredevil tactics (he was always at the front of his troops) cemented his reputation. After the defeat at Alamein, his brilliant retreat—in defiance of Hitler's direct orders—saved thousands of German lives.

In the weeks after D-day, Rommel confronted Hitler and boldly said what no one else in the Third Reich dared to: that the war was lost and Germany should seek peace terms. He was party to the failed July 20 assassination attempt on Hitler; two months later, in Ulm, he took his son aside and said, "I shall be dead in a quarter of an hour. Hitler is charging me with high treason. In view of my services in Africa I am to have the chance of dying by poison. In a quarter of an hour you will receive a call from the hospital in Ulm to say that I've had a brain seizure ... " Fifteen minutes later, the telephone rang.

0300-0400 Hours

Night Raids

SITUATION REPORT **Omaha/Gold/Juno Beaches** Transport ships (from, respectively, Task Forces O, G and J) arrive off the coast of Normandy and begin off-loading invasion troops to smaller landing craft • **Sword Beach** British glider troops establish a field headquarters at Ranville; new glider landings bring in the 6th Division's heavy weapons • **The Enemy** Reports of paratrooper and glider landings continue to filter in, but they are so scattered and fragmentary that they only confuse the Germans

---

FLYING COLORS: We can't show a picture of the night raids over France; there are none. These Martin B-26 Marauder bombers, en route to hit Cherbourg, sport the design motif all Allied aircraft used on D-day

A T 0330 HOURS ON JUNE 6, THE SKIES ABOVE ENGLAND, Normandy and the English Channel were buzzing and rumbling with traffic. In the late hours of June 5 and early on June 6, a gigantic Allied air armada— 3,467 heavy bombers, 1,645 medium bombers and 5,409 fighters—took to the skies from the scores of aerodromes hastily constructed across England in the past few years. Many air crews made two runs, some made three: Allied planes flew more than 14,000 sorties on D-day. The Royal Air Force led the action, bombing the Normandy coast and Caen at midnight. In the morning, with dawn beginning to show, U.S. Eighth Air Force planes hit the beaches, aiming to take out German guns and addle German gunners just before the first troops left the landing boats below. The big bombers, medium bombers and their fighter escorts had company, for more than 800 U.S. C-47s (Douglas DC-3s adapted for military use) were also in the air that night, carrying Allied paratroopers to their drops over Normandy, then returning to England.

In a later chapter, "The Airmen," we examine the strategy and performance of the Allied air forces on D-day. In this chapter, we pause simply to marvel at the diversity of the planes they flew. Only 41 years after the first successful powered flight, the airplane had completely changed the face of warfare; highly specialized aircraft filled the skies on D-day. High above were the big bombers, the U.S. B-17s and B-24s and the British Avro Lancasters. Beneath them flew medium-altitude bombers like the B-26 Marauders shown below. Initial-

ly plagued by problems, the Marauder later became a beloved workhorse and did good service on D-day; it had the lowest loss rate during the war of any U.S. bomber. Protecting the big bombers were such varied interceptor fighters as the U.S. P-38 and P-47 and the British Typhoon. German gunners called the Lockheed P-38 *der gabelschwanz teufel* ("the fork-tailed devil"), because of its unusual three-part body design.

Over the Channel on D-day flew other exotic birds: the British hunted subs and patrolled the sea lanes with the lumbering Catalina and the Swordfish, a biplane. Some U.S. landing craft came ashore carrying small Piper Cub airplanes to be used for reconnaissance and forward artillery spotting. Not present were U.S. Navy planes; Navy pilots flew a fascinating array of bombers, fighters and dive-bombers from their big aircraft carriers in the Pacific theater, but D-day was primarily the U.S. Army's show in the sky (the Air Force was not yet a separate branch of the U.S. military; all air operations on D-day were flown by the Army Air Force). Another air force was conspicuous by its absence in the historic hours of D-day: Adolf Hitler's once-threatening Luftwaffe had been so heavily battered by Allied air power by 1944 that Hermann Göring's pilots played almost no defensive role when Fortress Europe was attacked from the air. ■

JUNE 6, 1944

"Now we're on our bomb run and another of our ships takes a direct hit, blows up and goes down. Damn that briefer and his 'milk run.' What's with all this flak?"

—Lieut. J.K. Havener, B-26 co-pilot

AIR ARMADA

Less than 48 hours before the invasion, General Eisenhower issued an order that every Allied plane flying on D-day be painted with a motif of black and white stripes. Why? Per his written directive: "The object of this memorandum is to prescribe the distinctive marking which will be applied to U.S. and British aircraft to make them more easily identified as friendly by ground and naval forces and by other friendly aircraft."

B-24 Liberator ▲

Nation U.S.
Class Long-Range Heavy Bomber
Builder Consolidated Vultee (Convair)
Ceiling/Speed/Range 28,000 ft./290 mph/2,200 mi.
Crew Ten
Arms 8,000 lbs. of bombs, nine machine guns

P-38 Lightning ▲

Nation U.S.
Class Single-Seat, Long-Range Fighter
Builder Lockheed
Ceiling/Speed/Range 44,000 ft./414 mph/2,260 mi.
Crew One
Arms 4 cannon, 4 machine guns, 4,000 lbs. of bombs or ten rockets

Spitfire ►

Nation Britain
Class Fighter
Builder Supermarine
Ceiling/Speed/Range 37,000 ft./369 mph/1, 135 miles
Crew One
Arms Up to eight machine guns, four cannon, 1,000 lbs. of bombs

Lancaster ►

Nation Britain
Class Heavy Bomber
Builder Avro
Ceiling/Speed/Range 24,500 ft./287 mph/1,660 mi.
Crew Seven
Arms 22,000 lbs. of bombs, ten machine guns

TIME graphic by Lon Tweeten

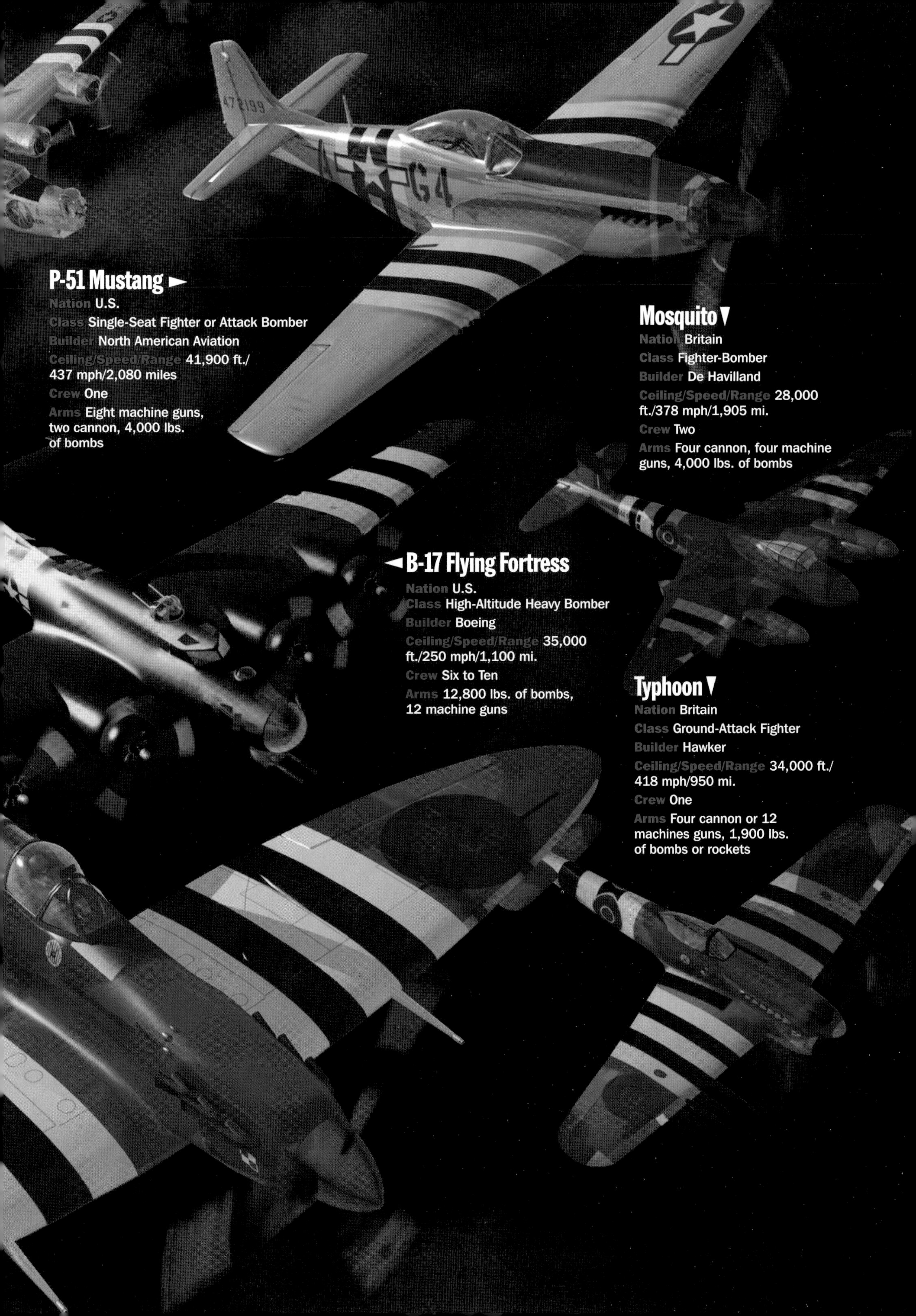

P-51 Mustang ►

Nation U.S.
Class Single-Seat Fighter or Attack Bomber
Builder North American Aviation
Ceiling/Speed/Range 41,900 ft./ 437 mph/2,080 miles
Crew One
Arms Eight machine guns, two cannon, 4,000 lbs. of bombs

Mosquito ▼

Nation Britain
Class Fighter-Bomber
Builder De Havilland
Ceiling/Speed/Range 28,000 ft./378 mph/1,905 mi.
Crew Two
Arms Four cannon, four machine guns, 4,000 lbs. of bombs

◄ B-17 Flying Fortress

Nation U.S.
Class High-Altitude Heavy Bomber
Builder Boeing
Ceiling/Speed/Range 35,000 ft./250 mph/1,100 mi.
Crew Six to Ten
Arms 12,800 lbs. of bombs, 12 machine guns

Typhoon ▼

Nation Britain
Class Ground-Attack Fighter
Builder Hawker
Ceiling/Speed/Range 34,000 ft./ 418 mph/950 mi.
Crew One
Arms Four cannon or 12 machines guns, 1,900 lbs. of bombs or rockets

0400-0500 Hours

The Armada

SITUATION REPORT **Operation Neptune** Five naval strike forces have taken up position off the Normandy coast adjacent to the five invasion beaches ● **In the Channel** Troops of the first assault wave are climbing down net ladders into landing craft that will ferry them 11 miles to Omaha and Utah beaches ● **Airborne operations** Pegasus Bridge has been secured, and glider units from the U.S. 82nd and 101st Airborne divisions have begun landing on the western flank of the Normandy beaches

A T 4:45 A.M., A GRAY STEEL MASS NOT MUCH LARGER than a small whale emerged silently from the waves just a mile off the Normandy coast. The small craft, designated X23, was carrying a crew of five on a high-risk mission that was critical to the success of the landings that would follow. Clinging to the catwalk as the high seas washed over his craft, Royal Navy Lieutenant George Honour erected an an 18-ft. telescopic mast equipped with a light shining out to sea, a radio beacon and an echo sounder tapping a message for the ships that were following. At the same moment, 20 miles to the east, an identical submarine, code-named X20, was deploying the same equipment. For the next five hours, these two subs would be the guideposts for British and Canadian ships approaching Juno and Sword beaches. As the sun rose, they would also become stationary, plainly visible targets for the German gunners onshore.

The armada being guided to shore by X20, X23 and other similar craft was the largest ever assembled in the history of human conflict. More than 5,300 vessels had departed from various English ports in the previous 48 hours, gathering at "Area Z," south of the Isle of Wight, and then making for the coast of France in five assault groups organized according to the landing beaches. The convoy included a bombardment force of 174 battleships, cruisers and destroyers, more than 2,000 landing craft, plus thousands of specialized vessels: minesweepers, barges, maintenance vessels, supply ships and hospital tenders. The Allied navies were responsible for three principal tasks: providing long-range artillery support for the landings by firing the largest of their guns from positions well out at sea (this would be the job of battleships and cruisers, which were too large to approach the shore); transporting the soldiers of the invasion force to shore; and offering close artillery support to those soldiers by firing at specif-

ANCHORS AWEIGH! The great armada—at more than 5,300 ships, the largest ever assembled—steams out of British ports, bound for France. The barrage balloons tethered to each ship are a defensive tactic; they help keep German fighters from strafing the ships

NATIONAL ARCHIVES

"It's the invasion. There must be ten thousand ships out there. If you don't believe me, come up here and see for yourself." —German Major Werner Pluskat

ABANDON SHIP! Minesweepers led the Allied convoy, followed by battleships, destroyers and, finally, the transports. The minesweeper U.S.S. *Tide*, center, made it through D-day, but hit a German mine amidships on June 7 at 9:40 a.m. and sank shortly after this photo was taken

ic targets from close range (this would fall to the destroyers). These tasks were grouped under the heading Operation Neptune, under the command of British Admiral Sir Bertram Ramsay. The night before D-day, Ramsay had written in the diary he kept (against Navy regulations) that "I am under no delusion as to the risks involved in this most difficult of all operations ... We shall require all the help that God can give us and I cannot believe that this will not be forthcoming."

Pity (and, perhaps, envy) German Major Werner Pluskat, who peered through a slit in his pillbox on the Normandy

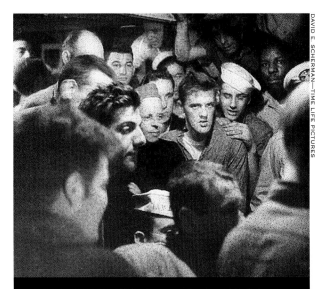

NOW HEAR THIS: LIFE photographer David E. Scherman captured U.S. sailors aboard LST 317 (Landing Ship, Tank) listening to orders from their skipper, piped belowdecks. The date: June 5, D-day minus one, as the ship was in mid-Channel, steaming toward France

coast the morning of June 6, stared into the dissipating predawn gloom, and saw a sight never to be seen again: an endless line of ships of every conceivable size, shape and description, stretching from horizon to horizon.

Just as the sun rose, the British cruiser H.M.S. *Belfast* added sound to the spectacle. At 5:30 a.m., she commenced firing her 14-in. guns at German coastal defenses above Gold Beach. Within minutes, nine more ships had opened fire at the same targets. At almost the same instant, 22 miles to the west, the U.S. destroyers *Fitch* and *Corry* opened fire on Utah Beach. They were joined within seconds by the U.S. cruisers *Quincy* and *Tuscaloosa*. A withering barrage of shells from 10-, 12- and 14-in. guns roared over the heads of British and American soldiers who were making for shore; many soldiers recall that their landing craft literally shook from the rush of air generated by the shells' passage. War correspondent Ernest Hemingway, aboard a landing craft, summed up the screaming racket: "It sounded as though they were throwing whole railway trains across the sky."

MANY OF THE LARGE BATTLESHIPS DEPLOYED IN Operation Neptune were nearly obsolete—of World War I vintage or earlier. These craft, such as the U.S.S. *Nevada* (commissioned in 1916, she was the only battleship to get under way at Pearl Harbor) and the H.M.S. *Rodney* (commissioned in 1927, she was the youngest of the battleships at D-day), could no longer engage modern battleships at sea but were still more than able to direct formidable firepower at German shore batteries. By the time D-day was over, the battleships had accomplished more direct hits against enemy positions—and to far better effect—than the repeated waves of Allied bombardment from the air.

But the truly critical role was played by destroyers. These vessels were small enough to approach within a mile of shore, where they could observe the action firsthand. Although destroyer captains had been ordered to stand down until forward observers were in place on shore to direct their fire, some—those observing the desperate plight of American Rangers on Omaha Beach, for example—could not restrain themselves. Lieutenant Commander Ralph Ramey, skipper of the destroyer U.S.S. *McCook*, took it upon himself to open fire on the pill-

Artifact

Neptune: Orders

On June 1, armed Allied messengers bore printed orders for Operation Neptune to the commander of each ship in the fleet. Inside two sealed envelopes were final orders for the vessel's role, as well as the date: June 5, with alternate dates of June 6 or 7. The message ended, "Destroy this by burning when you have read and understood." Someone defied the order, leaving history a copy.

boxes above Omaha Beach with his 5-in. guns. He provided the only coverage that the Rangers were getting that morning. Within minutes, an admiral stationed aboard a flagship farther out to sea realized what Ramey was accomplishing. He picked up a radio and bellowed, "Get on them, men! Get on them! They are raising hell with the men on the beach, and we can't have any more of that!" Instantly, every destroyer off Omaha Beach followed Ramey's lead, some skippers veering so close to shore that they risked running aground.

Naval historian Samuel Eliot Morison would later write that "this destroyer action against shore batteries afforded the troops the only artillery support they had during most of D-day." The actions of Ramey and other commanders like him not only saved countless lives but also prevented the Rangers at Omaha from being slaughtered or pushed back into the sea.

For all the risks and bravery that Operation Neptune entailed, its missions were accomplished both efficiently and at relatively little cost. Of the more than 5,300 ships, boats and amphibious craft that took part in the invasion, only about 200 were lost on June 6—and most of these were landing craft and other small vessels. Even the crews of X20 and X23 made it safely back to England. The help that Bertram Ramsay had predicted in his diary had indeed been forthcoming. ∎

Neptune's Commander

If the two worst things you can do in the military are contradict a superior and then turn out to be right, it's a wonder that Bertram Home Ramsay lasted more than a few months in the Royal Navy. As it was, this son of an army general enlisted at age 15 and was later among the first graduates of England's naval staff college. For much of his career, Ramsay showed talent and proficiency as an officer, persuading superiors to overlook his contrariness. By 1935, he had risen to rear admiral and was appointed chief of staff to the Home Fleet commander, Admiral Sir Roger Backhouse. It took Ramsay only three months to alienate Backhouse, who forced him to retire. As war approached, Ramsay was unofficially called out of retirement (his official status was still "inactive") and given the unglamorous command of Dover's coastal defenses. From this post, he repeatedly warned his chiefs that British forces, then reeling backward through France, might have to be evacuated from the Continent on a few days' notice. He was ignored but nonetheless managed to improvise the brilliant evacuation from Dunkirk when his predictions proved correct.

For this, Ramsay was knighted, but the Royal Navy still would not take him back. It was only after he was named to command Operation Neptune, Overlord's naval component, that Ramsay was officially restored to the active-duty list. While planning for D-day, he argued that heavily laden landing boats would not handle as easily in the rough waters of the English Channel as they did in the calm South Pacific. On June 6, countless lives were saved by his insistence that a greater number of landing boats than originally envisioned (each carrying a smaller load than SHAEF planners wanted) be assigned to the invasion. Ramsay, a little-sung hero of the invasion, died in a plane crash on Jan. 2, 1945.

OPEN FIRE! The big guns of the battleship U.S.S. *Nevada* pound the shore in the early-morning hours of June 6. Although the ship bombardment was far more accurate than Allied bombs, the German bunkers on the coast were so thick that many survived direct hits

JUNE 6, 1944

GOING IN: U.S. troops in a Higgins boat prepare to land on Omaha beach. With other boats and men already ashore, this is the second or third wave of landings

> "That s.o.b. Higgins. He ain't got nothin' to be proud of, inventing this boat." —Unknown soldier

0500-0600 Hours

Crossing the Channel

SITUATION REPORT Airborne Operations British paratroopers and glider troops have attacked and overrun the German gun emplacement at Merville. The village of Ste.-Mére-Eglise is under attack by American and British Airborne troops ● **French Resistance** German defenders within Ste.-Mére-Eglise are reporting that local communications have been disrupted ● **Omaha Beach** Naval bombardment is in progress as the first wave of amphibious duplex-drive tanks has begun moving toward shore

SARDINES: This transport ship, far larger than the small Higgins boats, will lower its front ramps to allow men and machines to move ashore

THE INFANTRY TROOPS BOBBING UP AND DOWN AT 0510 hours in the small boat designated LCC 60 "felt naked, defenseless," Howard Vander Beek would remember later. As they crossed the Channel in a convoy, there had at least been the feeling of safety in numbers. Now, more than 2,700 of the flat-bottomed landing craft known as Higgins boats (for the New Orleans shipyard owner who built them) huddled together in the dark—each emblazoned with a freshly painted, oversized letter: "O" for Omaha, "U" for Utah and so on. The convoy had split into five branches as the armada approached France, but there were still hundreds of Higgins boats in each group. And they were still sheltered by the larger destroyers and battleships that were escorting them to Normandy, still watched over by the fast-moving PT boats that darted in and out of the armada, looking for enemy activity on the water or in the sky.

But 10 minutes before sunlight first touched the eastern sky, even these smaller groups had fanned out into wide skirmish lines, riding the waves shoulder to shoulder, all facing toward the French shore, which was now just barely visible in the first light of day. By 0522, all the Higgins boats in the first landing wave had taken up what their orders called "beaching stations": positions in the water directly offshore from which they were supposed to hit the land, open their maws and disgorge their men.

And then, what must have seemed like a reprieve: while the Higgins boats held their positions, a wave of Allied bombers flew in over their heads, followed by a second and then a third. Each phalanx of heavy bombers dropped its full load either onto the beaches

in front of the landing vessels or immediately beyond—seeming to pulverize whatever lay waiting for the Allies on the beaches. Or so the men in the boats hoped.

Then the bombers receded; silence once again. Minutes later, the destroyers and battleships that had escorted the Higgins boats across the Channel but had not approached the shore opened up with their 5-, 10-, 12-, and 14-in. guns. The roar of these salvos passing overhead deafened the men in the landing boats; the rush of air created by the giant shells (which one awed infantryman compared to "the size of jeeps") and the more than 14,000 rockets fired at the invasion beaches caused the small Higgins boats to rise momentarily out of the water. Within seconds, the German gun batteries onshore answered.

As they watched this exchange, feeling for the moment more like observers than participants, many of the landing troops must have reflected that the war at last was upon them. TIME had captured their defiantly gay departure: "On the way to the boats in England, some of them had picked flowers, stuck them in their gun muzzles. One man carried a guitar, another wore a red & white sign on his back: DANGER—MINEFIELD."

Of the 156,000 Allied troops who would land in France on June 6, many had been aboard transport ships for a full week, while some units remained on land until June 5. Both British and American infantry, accustomed to cold field rations, were astonished by the good hot food served by the Navy. But as H-hour drew closer, few of them felt like eating. Although the night of June 5 and the early hours of June 6 were cold in the English Channel, many of the men sweated profusely. In the choppy waters, seasickness afflicted private and general alike; the men Dwight Eisenhower had summoned to a "great crusade" would go into battle reeking of vomit and reeling from nausea.

The hours passed; men steeled themselves for what they were about to face in different ways. Some gambled. Some prayed. Others rehearsed procedure in their minds one last time. Army Ranger Frank South, bound for Omaha Beach, repeatedly cleaned his .45 Colt automatic, sharpened his knife and mentally reviewed the plans and orders he had rehearsed countless times in the months leading up to D-day. And a few succumbed to nervous tension. One Ranger battalion com-

Artifact

Infantry Lifebelt

Inflated by hand, this belt was standard issue for landing troops. A TIME reporter noted other last-minute gear handed out to the soldiers: "Seven sticks of chewing gum, emergency rations, insecticide powder, cigarettes, a tin of canned heat, water-purification tablets, chewing tobacco, one razor blade, twelve seasickness pills, two vomit bags— which many of them used."

JACKSON HILL, COURTESY OF THE NATIONAL D-DAY MUSEUM

On the Verge

CLOCKWISE FROM TOP RIGHT: ROBERT HUNT LIBRARY; FRANK SCHERSCHEL—TIME LIFE PICTURES; DAVID E. SCHERMAN—TIME LIFE PICTURES; NATIONAL ARCHIVES; HULTON ARCHIVE—GETTY IMAGES; FRANK SCHERSCHEL—TIME LIFE PICTURES; ROBERT HUNT LIBRARY

Cards, chess, shuffleboard: anything to take the men's minds off the task that awaited them. LIFE photographer David Scherman, who took some of these photos, cabled back to the U.S.: "I sailed on an LST ... we were under way at 3:15 Monday morning in a rough sea. At 3:31 Tuesday morning we anchored and dropped our LC boats. Then we dropped our amphibious vehicles, known as 'ducks'" ... Our bow doors closed at H plus one and the skipper rubbed his hands and said, 'Well, let's go back to England.' We passed a craft ... a square-shaped, frame double-decker with six chimneys. [Our] signal officer said: 'Captain! What the hell is that piece of equipment?' On its side was painted LCK. We looked that up in the orders and it read, 'Landing Craft, Kitchen,' then promptly signaled them for 'a double malted, a ham on rye and forget the mustard.' Blinked back the six-chimneyed LCK steaming toward the beaches: 'Baloney!'"

THE GUY WHO RELAXES
IS HELPING THE AXIS!

ON THE DOUBLE: Urged on by a propaganda poster, workers in one of Higgins' seven factories in New Orleans churn out his landing boats

mander took took to drink, then began loudly predicting that the assault on Pointe du Hoc was sheer suicide. Soon he struck a senior office; he was arrested and returned to England.

THE TENSION HAD RISEN HOURS EARLIER, AT 0100, WHEN bosuns' whistles began to sound aboard the various transport ships in the Channel, followed by an announcement: "Now hear this! All assault troops report to your debarkation areas." This was the order to begin transferring men and machines from the larger ships to the landing craft that would ferry them to the beaches. Weighed down by hundreds of pounds of equipment, soldiers backed down rope ladders and scrambled on nets draped over the sides of the transport ships. Others were ordered to jump from the deck of the larger ship to the landing craft below; dozens of bones were broken. Several soldiers were crushed between the hull of a transport and the side of a landing craft bobbing beside it. A better idea: some boats on larger ships were filled first, then simply lowered over the side. One of these became snared on the sides of the British transport *Empire Javelin*, just below the huge sewage outlet from the ship's toilets. For the 20 minutes to took to free the landing craft, Major Thomas Dallas and members of the 29th Division were drenched in

the steady flow from the heads. Welcome to France, gentlemen!

Now the whistle sounded again, followed by the order, "Away all boats!" As each landing boat pushed away from its transport ship, it began circling, while other boats tied up and took on troops and gear. The circles traced by the departing craft drew ever wider and finally arced toward the Normandy coast. Within the landing craft, men stood pressed against one another. There were usually 30 to each Higgins boat, sometimes fewer when heavy equipment like a jeep was packed aboard. By 0500, nearly all of the infantry who would assault the five invasion beaches had been loaded into the 2,727 landing craft that would bear them toward the shore, and those assigned to the first wave had taken up positions facing the beach.

In open water, no longer sheltered by the larger ships, the Higgins boats began to pitch and roll. "That s.o.b. Higgins," historian Samuel Eliot Morison would later quote one drenched, seasick soldier as saying. "He ain't got nothin' to be proud of, inventing this boat!" But as the naval barrage lifted and the Higgins boats at last began to churn at full speed toward the beaches of Normandy, those inside would, in a few short minutes, remember fondly the comparative safety and comfort of an open-topped boat rising and falling with the swells of the English Channel in the middle of the night. ∎

The Man Behind the Boats

Eisenhower called him "the man who won the war for us." Hitler called him "the new Noah." They were both referring to the hard-charging, tough-talking boat designer whose innovative flat-bottomed landing craft cleared the way for the amphibious landings at Normandy and other beachheads during World War II: Andrew J. Higgins.

A Higgins boat with a hinged prow could rush onto a beach, disgorge men and equipment and then back straight out again. The craft changed the nature of warfare: seaborne assaults, which had always required harbors, now could be mounted against almost any shoreline in the world. Without Higgins boats, Eisenhower would later say, "we could never have landed over an open beach. The whole strategy of the war would have been different." One of the reasons Ike waited until June to launch D-day was to have the benefit of an extra month of production of Higgins boats, which by 1944 were coming out of the factory at the rate of 700 a month.

The Higgins design, however obvious in retrospect, was considered radical at a time when the Navy was fixated on vessels with V-shaped hulls. In addition to its flat bottom, the boat offered other innovations. Its propeller was recessed in a tube, protecting it from scraping the bottom and keeping the boat's draw to a minimum. A concave curvature in the midsection of the hull improved the craft's hydrodynamics. The vessel could thus slide on its belly over almost any submerged obstacle and needed little more than its own length to turn around. And it was speedy, making better than 20 knots in knee-deep water.

That Higgins' innovations were slow to find acceptance perhaps owed more to his lack of diplomatic skill than to flaws in his work. He once walked into a meeting with Navy chieftains, wrote the words "this boat stinks" across the blueprint of a new design under review, and stalked out. During a wartime visit to the White House, he blithely told President Roosevelt (a former Assistant Secretary of the Navy), "You don't know the front end of a boat from the back end."

But Higgins was also a earnest patriot who once demanded that the Navy reopen negotiations on a contract that had already been signed, in order to pay him less, because he felt it was unseemly to make too much money while American boys were dying in combat. He was also an inspiring leader who would stage his own version of fireside chats, speaking to his army of 20,000 employees over a public address system wired into the seven New Orleans factories that were making Higgins boats by 1943.

Most of all, though, he was a visionary. When the Navy asked him early in the war to come up with a new design for a landing craft that could carry a tank, Higgins agreed but didn't bother with producing a set of blueprints. Instead, he built the actual boat and delivered it— 61 hours later. By September 1943, the Navy had a total inventory of 14,072 vessels. Of that number, 12,964—or 92% of the entire fleet—were designed or built by Higgins Industries.

Boat design was not the only area in which Higgins was forward-looking. He willingly hired women and African Americans, then scandalized the South by paying them the same high wages he offered to white men. He did the same for his elderly and disabled workers.

When news of the D-day landings reached the home front, Higgins was in Chicago. He drafted a telegram to be read to his workers in New Orleans. It declared, "This is the day for which we have been waiting. Now, the work of our hands, our hearts and our heads is being put to the test. We may all be inspired by the news that the first landings on the continent were made by the Allies in our boats."

Artifact

Higgins Helmet

This isn't a helmet worn by troops on D-day; it's a hardhat donned by workers in the Higgins boat factories to protect themselves on the assembly line. Like many of the artifacts shown in this book, the helmet is part of the permanent collection of the National D-Day Museum in New Orleans.

The Higgins Factor

Born in 1886, the youngest in a Nebraska family of 10 children, Andrew J. (for Jackson) Higgins (at right, above) exhibited an early flair as an entrepreneur. At age 9, he began cutting grass with a sickle. He then purchased a lawn mower with his earnings, then another; soon he was supervising 17 mowers, mostly boys older than himself. At age 12, Higgins offered two hints of his future: he built a full-size boat in his parent's basement. Then, when he realized that the craft was too large to fit through any doorway in the house, he waited until his mother left on an errand, took out the back wall of the basement and moved the boat outside. He was rebricking the wall when his mother returned.

By the time he was 20, Higgins, who had worked in Wyoming logging camps, moved to Alabama to start a timber company. The business flourished but was wiped out by a hurricane. Undaunted, Higgins relocated to New Orleans in 1916 and cast his eye on the plentiful but difficult-to-harvest timber in Louisiana's bayous. He adapted a Dutch design for a flat-bottomed boat, added a recessed propeller to ride over submerged tree stumps and got rich felling trees other lumbermen couldn't reach. Soon he was selling vessels to both Prohibition-era rumrunners and the federal agents who chased them.

By the late 1930s, Higgins counted among his clients the Coast Guard, the Army Corps of Engineers and the U.S. Geological Survey—but not the U.S. Navy, which didn't see a need for his ugly, boxy, flat-bottomed boats. Urged on by Marine Corps top brass, already bracing for island war in the Pacific, the Navy reluctantly reconsidered and gave Higgins' boats a tryout on Lake Ponchartrain in May 1941. Amazed by the versatility of his design, the Navy soon ordered the first of what would become a production run of 20,094 boats.

SITUATION REPORT Utah Beach First wave of assault troops begins landing—but not at their intended location. In contrast to the developing situation at Omaha, U.S. boats at Utah launch amphibious tanks close to shore; only four sink • Sword Beach Naval bombardment of coastal gun emplacements begins • Gold/Juno Beaches Assault troops are disembarking from transport ships and loading onto the landing craft that will take them to the shore • Aerial Bombardment Another bombing raid on Caen begins

JUNE 6, 1944

ROBERT BIXLER, A NATIVE OF SHAMOKIN, PA., HAD IT all planned. "I'm going to land with a comb in one hand and a pass to Paris in the other," he had joked a few hours earlier, as he and other members of D Company, 116th Infantry Regiment, 29th Division, climbed from the British transport *Empire Javelin* down into the landing craft that would bring them ashore at the beach Operation Overlord planners had dubbed Omaha. At about the same time, Ray Stevens and his twin brother Roy, both of A Company, were preparing to climb into their landing vessels. Ray extended his hand to his brother, but Roy refused to shake it, saying, "I'll shake your hand in Vierville"—referring to the village their unit was slated to capture—"later this morning sometime." The confidence of men like Bixler and the Stevens brothers reflected the view, widely shared among infantrymen in both the 1st Division and the 29th (the two units that would land at this four-mile stretch of sand between Pointe du Hoc in the west and the town of Ste.-Honorine-des-Petres in the east), that Omaha was going to be easy.

The troops of the 1st and 29th Divisions had been assured, after all, that the Air Force was going to pulverize the German beach defenses on Omaha hours before they landed. And what the bombers missed, the Navy would get, in a second wave of fire that would end just minutes before the first troops hit the beach. Not that there was much to hit: in the summer of 1943, D-day planners had chosen Omaha as one of the five invasion beaches because it was almost completely undefended. They were right—at the time. But General Erwin Rommel later heavily strengthened the Atlantic Wall defenses on the coast. Yet just one month before the invasion, Allied intelligence still was reporting scant fortifications, sparsely manned by understrength German units, composed mostly of POWs from countries Germany had conquered. Even if the fighting was heavier than expected, intelligence briefers had told the troops, the craters left by the air and naval bombardments would dot the beach with scores of ready-made foxholes.

And even if the terrain (one of the world's widest tidal flats, which ended at the foot of a bluff that reached more than 100 ft. skyward) seemed to offer natural advantages to a dug-

HORROR: Photographer Robert Capa landed with the first wave at the Easy Red/Fox Green sector of Omaha Beach, where he recorded desperate U.S. troops, under fire, taking shelter behind "hedgehogs" after landing

ROBERT CAPA—MAGNUM PHOTOS

"Get these men the hell off this beach! Go kill some goddamn Krauts!" —Colonel Charles Canham

in defender, Bixler, the Stevens brothers and the thousands of other troops who were now steaming toward shore could count on the tanks. The plan called for dozens of duplex-drive (DD) amphibious tanks to land on Omaha before the first infantry set foot there and flatten whatever resistance the Germans tried to mount. For all of these reasons, Overlord planners had chosen to make Omaha the beach where the vast majority of U.S. troops and supplies would land on D-day. And for the same reasons, the rank and file had come to believe that Omaha would be, in the words of Sergeant Bob Slaughter of D Company, "a walk-in."

NOW, AS THEIR LANDING CRAFT CAME WITHIN SIGHT OF the beach at 0630, Slaughter, Bixler and the Stevens twins were no longer so sure. Certainly, the naval artillery barrage that had just ended looked and sounded like more than enough to crush any German presence on the beach. But German batteries onshore that the landing troops hadn't expected to be there were now answering the destroyers and battleships in the Channel in kind, seemingly unscathed by the bombardments from air and sea.

"Where are the tanks?" wondered many of the troops as they drew so close to the beach that German gunners stopped firing at the large vessels farther offshore and turned their attention to the landing craft. The infantrymen had no way of knowing it, but the wave of amphibious tanks that had been scheduled to precede them had gone missing in action. In the confusion caused by the bad weather that marked the first

hours of June 6, these tanks had been released too early and too far from shore by the ships that had borne them across the Channel. Barely seaworthy in calm conditions and shallow water, the tanks were no match for high seas and heavy weather. Of the 32 amphibious tanks that headed off toward shore, 27 sank before they got close to the beach. A handful made it ashore, but most of them were burning wrecks by the time the first troops stepped onto the sand.

Nor were tanks the only wreckage. Drawing to within 1,000 yds. of the waterline, the men of D Company could now see the first handful of landing craft that had started for shore ahead of them. As these boats touched shore and lowered their ramps, they had been raked by machine-gun fire and mortar shells from the tops of the Omaha bluffs. Whole companies had been wiped out in seconds. On several boats, particularly those that had carried the men of Companies A and B, everyone aboard seemed to have been killed before a single man could step onto the sand. In the space of a few minutes, the confident banter about meeting atop the Omaha bluffs and visiting Paris turned to something closer to pure terror. "Man," Slaughter said numbly to a soldier standing beside him, "we're going to catch hell."

"The plan is nothing …" General Dwight D. Eisenhower had been fond of reminding his staff in the months leading up to June 6. He knew too well that elaborately choreographed combat scenarios could disintegrate into incoherence amid the chaos of battle. And so it was at Omaha Beach. The bluffs that were supposed to be lightly fortified turned out to be

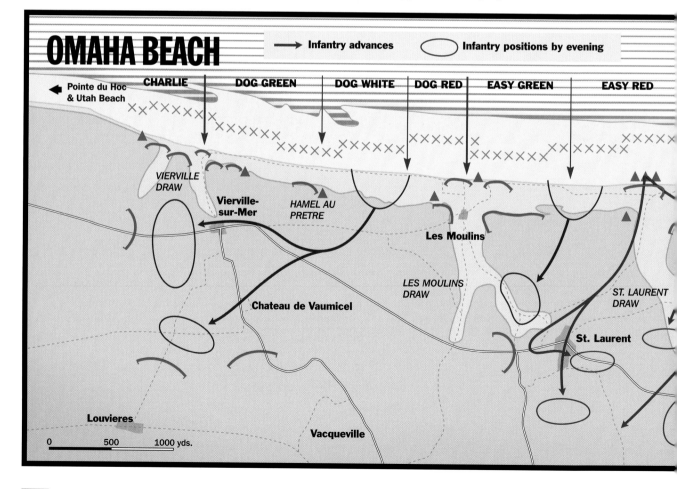

OMAHA BEACH → Infantry advances ⬭ Infantry positions by evening

◄ Pointe du Hoc & Utah Beach · CHARLIE · DOG GREEN · DOG WHITE · DOG RED · EASY GREEN · EASY RED

VIERVILLE DRAW
Vierville-sur-Mer
HAMEL AU PRETRE
Les Moulins
LES MOULINS DRAW
ST. LAURENT DRAW
Chateau de Vaumicel
St. Laurent
Louvieres
Vacqueville

0 — 500 — 1000 yds.

honeycombed with 85 machine-gun nests, 38 rocket emplacements, 35 pillboxes, 18 antitank gun positions, eight fortified gun batteries, six mortar pits and four field artillery positions—all linked by an extensive network of trenches. The single regiment of demoralized foreign troops thought to be defending Omaha turned out to be an entire division of young, professional soldiers from Germany's heartland, many of them battle-hardened veterans of the Russian front. (A secret study conducted by Eisenhower's staff in early 1944 had concluded that the presence of a full division would make Omaha "impregnable.") Because most of the amphibious tanks had never reached the shore, the long-planned vision for the landing—that mobile armored units would charge up the four "draws," the heavily defended ravines that provided a path for men and equipment from the beach to the top of the bluffs—now seemed impossible.

But the men of D Company and those who hit the shore in the minutes after 0630 knew none of this. "Where are the craters?" the men now wondered, as they sprinted from the ramps of their landing craft through a withering blizzard of bullets and shrapnel. The troops were desperately in need of cover, but the bomb-crater foxholes they had been told to expect were nowhere to be found. The problem was that Air Force bombers assigned to Omaha, blinded by early-morning cloud cover, had erred on the side of caution (wanting to avoid hitting Allied troops near the beach) and paused an extra few seconds before releasing their loads. So the bombs intended to wreck Omaha's defenses and crater its beaches had instead slaughtered French farm animals (and yes, some Allied paratroopers) in pastures a few miles behind the bluffs. Similarly, the naval bombardment that followed was mostly off the mark—again owing to limited visibility caused by the weather.

Without tanks, without shelter and facing much stronger opposition than they had expected, the troops of the 1st and 29th Divisions had but one grim advantage: there were so many of them that it was impossible for the Germans to shoot everyone at once. As the first trickle of landing craft gave way to dozens, then more than

Hero of Omaha Beach

Standing tall when everyone around him was ducking for cover, strolling along the beach amid a constant spray of bullets with a cane in one hand and a cigar of Churchillian proportions in the other, General Norman Cota seemed to the troops on Omaha Beach to be as much an apparition as an inspiration.

"I thought he was crazy," recalled Pete Cardinali, then a 20-year-old sergeant with the 5th Ranger Battalion. "Nothing had prepared me for the terrible shooting all around, all the bodies, all the death. The situation seemed disastrous. Then I saw General Cota, standing up, waving his .45, trying to get his troops off the beach." Coming upon Cardinali's unit, Cota uttered four words that became immortal: "Rangers, lead the way!" As Cardinali recalled, "We all passed the word down the line: 'Rangers, let's go!' We headed over the seawall and started up a grassy bluff. We made our way to the top under heavy fire." Cota's phrase later became the Rangers' official motto.

Born in Chelsea, Mass., in 1893, Cota attended West Point, graduating in 1917. He helped organize the invasions of North Africa and Sicily, and by late 1943, as planning for Overlord heated up, he was regarded as the Army's foremost expert on amphibious landings in Europe. Today Cota is remembered as much for what he probably didn't say on D-day as for what he did. The movie version of *The Longest Day* has Robert Mitchum (playing Cota) yelling to panicked troops on Omaha, "Only two kinds of people are gonna stay on this beach: those that are already dead and those that are gonna die. Now get off your butts! You guys are the Fighting 29th!" But a number of witnesses claim that a slightly less screenwriterly version of those words was used by Colonel George Taylor, who was standing near Cota as the troops were inspired to charge up the bluffs. Norman Cota died in 1971.

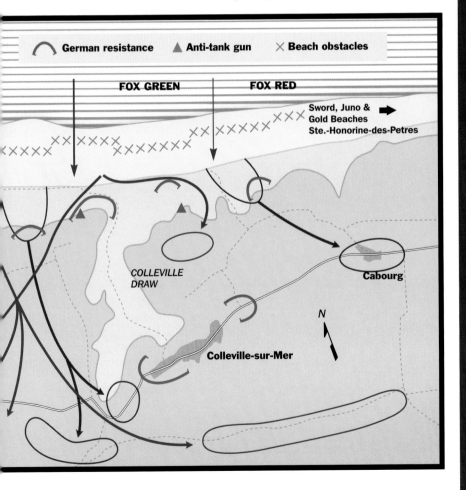

German resistance ⌒   ▲ Anti-tank gun   ✕ Beach obstacles

FOX GREEN   FOX RED

Sword, Juno & Gold Beaches ➡
Ste.-Honorine-des-Petres

COLLEVILLE DRAW

Cabourg

N

Colleville-sur-Mer

100, small handfuls of troops were able to scramble away from their Higgins boats before being hit. For some, like P.F.C. Robert Sales, a radio operator with B Company, it was simply a matter of luck. Sales tripped on the ramp of his landing craft while disembarking, which took him out of the line of fire of a machine gun that opened up a fraction of a second later, killing everyone else on the boat. Sales, like everyone else who managed to reach land alive, sprinted across the wide beach for the seawall at the base of the bluff.

During the first 60 minutes following H-hour (0630) on Omaha, several hundred American troops managed to survive the ordeal of coming ashore. But this created a new problem: without tanks to lead them up the heavily fortified draws, these troops had no place to go. Remaining on the beach, even huddled at the seawall or beneath the bluffs, left them undefended against the fire raining down from above and the side, while creating so much congestion that subsequent waves of troops would be stalled at the waterline, where the Germans had the best opportunity to slaughter them.

In the weeks before D-day, when Eisenhower would remind his staff that "the plan is nothing," he would sometimes add a related thought: "… but the planning is everything." Ike

DAZED AND CONFUSED: Wounded soldiers of the 116th Infantry Regiment take shelter beneath the chalk cliffs near the beach as they await evacuation from Omaha

believed that the endless process of drilling, training and anticipating contingencies would help troops take the initiative even when the plan was inoperative. He was right: pure, gutsy initiative would save the day at Omaha.

A T 0730, A LANDING BOAT CARRYING GENERAL NORMAN Cota of the 29th Division came ashore. Dodging fire, the 51-year-old general sprinted across the beach to the seawall, where he picked up a discarded machine gun, sprayed the top of the bluffs with fire and began to rally the disorganized troops. Because the infantrymen were carrying only light weapons, Cota realized that there was little hope of taking the draws that had been Omaha's original objective. So he discarded that plan and improvised a new one on the spot: the troops would bypass the draws by climbing directly up the bluffs, which were less heavily defended. And they would do it with Cota himself in the lead. Using bangalore torpedoes (small explosives) to blast barbed-wire obstacles, Cota and a

DOWN: In the first few grim hours on Omaha, there was no time to care for the dead. But by nightfall, with U.S. control established, bodies were given temporary burial

small group reached the top of the bluff in less than an hour.

As more troops followed Cota up the bluff, the deadly traffic jam on the beach below started to ease ever so slightly. But new troops were still landing faster than they were leaving the beach, and the swelling, slow-moving crowds offered German snipers and artillerymen numerous targets. By 0830, Navy officers near the beach concluded that continued landings were making the situation worse. So they ordered their landing craft to stop ferrying troops to Omaha.

Farther out in the Channel, aboard the U.S.S. *Augusta*, General Omar Bradley, commander of U.S. forces on both Omaha and Utah beaches, was seriously worried. By 0900, almost 5,000 men were ashore, along with dozens of vehicles. As far as Bradley could tell (he had no way of knowing about Cota's progress), they were all stranded on the beach, in the crosshairs of German gunners. He began to weigh the possibility of canceling the landings at Omaha and diverting to Utah Beach all U.S. troops who had not yet gone ashore. But

Bradley was deeply reluctant to do this, knowing that he had no way to evacuate the men who had already landed, and that such a decision would condemn thousands of Americans to capture or death at the hands of the Germans.

Meanwhile, at the top of the Omaha bluff, Cota led his growing contingent of troops into the village of Vierville, slightly more than a quarter-mile in from the beach; they found it undefended. After capturing the town, Cota doubled back toward the beach, hoping that the advantage of surprise would compensate for the lack of tanks and enable him to capture the Vierville Draw (which connected the village to the beach) and some of the fortified positions that surrounded it. Because the attention of the draw's German defenders was focused entirely on the beach below, they didn't realize that Cota and his troops were approaching them from the rear— until it was too late. Within an hour, Cota and troops from the 116th Regiment (of which D Company was a part) had overrun the Vierville Draw, driving out, capturing or killing all the Germans who had been stationed within. Although it would take another eight hours for engineers to clear the draw of mines, the tide of the battle had begun to turn.

On the beach below, the situation remained desperate.

While a small number of Americans were now moving over the bluff, several thousand remained stranded and vulnerable. Because the Navy had ceased landing operations, these troops were cut off from both reinforcement and retreat. And they were being methodically butchered by the German gunners above. All of this was being observed, with mounting fury, by the crews of U.S. Navy destroyers stationed several miles off Omaha beach. They were close enough to watch the carnage but too far away to fire with sufficient accuracy to be sure of hitting the enemy and not U.S. troops. Adding to their frustration, the destroyer commanders had been ordered to remain clear of the beach, so as not to interfere with landing craft and to avoid the risk of running aground in shallow water.

Finally, the skipper of the U.S.S. *McCook* decided that he could no longer stand by and watch the grisly spectacle without acting. Defying orders, Lieut. Commander Ralph Ramey drove the *McCook* toward shore at full speed, unleashing the ship's 5-in. guns at German positions above the beach from point-blank range. Minutes later, every destroyer off Omaha followed Ramey's lead, launching a blistering fusillade at enemy strongpoints. Within 30 minutes, half a dozen German gun emplacements had been destroyed, and the rate of fire from the top of the bluff slowed considerably. For the second time at Omaha Beach on D-day, a commander had followed Ike's dictum, torn up the plans and seized the initiative. In response, one of the few working radios on Omaha was used to transmit the message, "Thank God for the United States Navy."

AT THE SEAWALL, COLONEL CHARLES CANHAM, COMMANDER of the 116th Regiment, used the respite from German fire to rally more troops into a charge over the bluff. Waving a .45 in his left hand (because he had been shot in his right), Canham raced along the seawall, bellowing, "Get these men the hell off this beach! Go kill some goddamn krauts!" To a U.S. officer he found hiding in a bunker abandoned by the Germans, Canham thundered, "Get your ass out of there and show some leadership!" Now the slow migration of troops over the bluff turned into a dam burst, as hundreds of infantry charged over the dunes, linked up with Cota and his men at the top and began overrunning German positions.

On the beach, as crowding cleared and German fire slackened, the few U.S. vehicles that had landed successfully went into action. Bulldozers began clearing a path through barbed-wire obstructions at the base of a second draw, which led to the

0730: Framed by two Americans in steel helmets and life jackets, U.S. soldiers in the second wave of landings wade through rough seas to land on the shore. One in 18 men who landed at Omaha Beach died on D-day, but the percentage of fatalities was far higher for the courageous troops in the initial assault

towns of St. Laurent and Colleville. By 1300, this St. Laurent Draw had been cleared of Germans, and troops, armor and equipment were moving up it to the plateau above the beach.

Although the order prohibiting further troop landings was still in effect, by 1100 the beach had begun to clear up. Several landing craft commanders who had been circling for hours offshore ignored the order to halt the landings and seized the chance to drive their boats onto the beach. Their successful landings inspired both the troops already ashore (who were heartened by the prospect of supply and reinforcement) and other Higgins boat commanders, who quickly resumed landings. As fewer and fewer German gun emplacements were still able to fire, this wave of troops and equipment, including tanks, reached shore largely unmolested. At the beach, momentum had been restored. On the bluffs above, the initiative now belonged to the Americans.

Noon passed. Aboard the *Augusta*, a heartsick Omar Bradley (who had not yet received word of the change in the battle's direction) was still leaning toward abandoning Omaha Beach. Everything seemed to have gone wrong at the single most critical Allied landing site. But at 1309, he received the message that changed his mind: "Troops formerly pinned down … advancing up heights behind beaches." At that moment, Bradley would later write, "I gave up any thought of abandoning Omaha Beach." Within three hours, the Colleville Draw, the third of the four draws leading from the beach to the top of the bluffs, was in American hands. (The fourth draw, near Les Moulins, would not be cleared of Germans until 2000.)

For the Germans at Omaha, the day grew bleaker with each passing hour. Even the staunchest and luckiest among the defenders could hope to hold off the American advance only for as long as their ammunition held out. But Allied air supremacy meant that they could not expect to be resupplied or reinforced. The last German resistance at the beachhead was subdued by the evening, around 2230. By that time, more than 30,000 American troops had come ashore at Omaha. But the beachhead had commanded a price in blood: more than 2,000 Americans died on the landing site they had expected would be "a walk-in." Among them was Ray Stevens. Years later, his twin brother Roy—who had refused to shake Ray's hand, so sure was he that the two would meet atop the bluffs over Omaha in a few short hours—would remember wistfully, "Man, we were so confident. We were going to whip them and still be home for Christmas." ∎

JUNE 1944

"Located Pointe du Hoc. Mission accomplished.
Need ammunition and reinforcements. Many casualties."
—Message sent via signal lamp by Colonel James Rudder, D-day

Pointe du Hoc

SITUATION REPORT **Omaha Beach** Second wave of troops landing; first advances made over the bluffs
• **Gold Beach** First and second waves of British troops land; second wave takes heavy casualties from
German fire at Le Hamel strongpoint • **Juno Beach** First and second waves of Canadian troops go ashore
• **Sword Beach** First wave of British troops and French commandos goes ashore and begins moving
off the beach • **Operation Neptune** The destroyer U.S.S. *Corry* hits a submerged mine and is disabled

JAMES RUDDER WAS RUNNING LATE. THE U.S. ARMY RANGER colonel, assigned to lead three companies in an assault against an isolated German gun emplacement, had been held up when the British coxswains piloting his landing boats allowed a tidal current to carry them two miles east of his target. When Rudder realized the snafu, he ordered them to come about and make for his actual objective, a jagged promontory of rock jutting into the sea between Omaha and Utah beaches. But fighting the current took more than 40 minutes, during which Rudder's flotilla was subjected to withering fire from German coastal gunners, sinking one of his four amphibious armored vehicles. To add to his woes, two of his LCAs (Landing Craft Assault) had foundered earlier in the assembly area off the coast, leaving him both short-handed and minus half his essential supplies. Colonel James Rudder wasn't happy.

And Pointe du Hoc, where Rudder and his Rangers landed at 0710, was not a good place to arrive without a full complement of men and matériel. Indeed, it was a place at which most soldiers would prefer never to arrive at all. Not so much a beach as a narrow strip of sand at the base of a 100-ft. cliff—at the top of which squatted heavy gun batteries and nearly impregnable concrete fortifications—Pointe du Hoc was very likely the single least inviting of the D-day landing grounds.

But Rudder's mission was among the most important of the morning: the six 155-mm artillery pieces that Allied intelligence had detected at Pointe du Hoc were more than capable of butchering all the forces that would come ashore on Omaha and Utah beaches and sinking much of the Allied armada in the Channel. If the cliffs were not scaled and those guns not silenced, the entire American sector of the invasion might be repelled, and Operation Overlord itself would be in jeopardy.

The Rangers' scheduled 0630 arrival had been timed to coincide precisely with the end of a heavy naval barrage from

the battleship U.S.S. *Texas*, which would have kept Pointe du Hoc's German defenders huddled in their bunkers. As it was, the enemy had more than enough time to regroup and open fire on the approaching Rangers. Meanwhile, Rudder's assault force had been promised a 500-man backup team, which had been ordered to wait offshore and watch for a signal flare from Rudder at 0700, indicating the cliffs had been scaled. When boats were late and the signal didn't come, the support team was reassigned to Omaha Beach.

A final barrier: the morning tide had started to come in beneath the Pointe's cliffs while the invaders were off-course, thus providing much less landing space than Rudder had expected. What little room he could see ahead consisted mostly of water-slick rock. So the unit's amphibious vehicles—upon which were mounted the 75-ft. mechanized ladders that the Rangers planned to use to scale the cliffs—couldn't gain enough traction to emerge from the surf.

Rudder's LCA would be the first to land. As it approached the beach, the Ranger colonel decided not to use the ladders; instead, he deployed his six rocket guns, which fired steel grappling hooks tethered to rope ladders and climbing lines. Once ashore, Rudder's men fired them straight up the cliff, and although many of the hooks failed to reach the top of the cliff, half a dozen or so snared on barbed wire or found a hold in the craggy rock at the top.

And here, at last, Rudder's luck turned: the intense aerial and naval bombardment in the days leading up to June 6 had destabilized the wall of stone and clay that faced the ocean at Pointe du Hoc, and a huge section of the cliff face had fallen into the surf below. At some points, the resulting large mound of rock and spoil reduced by as much as half the distance that the Rangers would have to ascend.

From the moment the Rangers stepped ashore, they were raked by machine-gun and sniper fire from German pillboxes. First Sergeant Leonard Lomell, then 24 and an acting platoon leader, would later tell TIME that "as I was getting off, I was shot in my side, but the bullet only went through muscle—it didn't hit any joints—so I was able to keep going. When you're a leader, you've got to see to it that everything gets done. As long as you can stand up, you keep going. After get-

GETTING THE POINTE: Douglas A-20 attack bombers soften up the prominent Pointe du Hoc prior to June 6. In the five weeks before D-day, bombers of the U.S. Ninth Air Force flew thousands of sorties against the Germans

IN CHARGE: Atop the Pointe, Rangers set up shop in a bunker, while German prisoners are led away. The flag is on display to signal Allied planes to hold their bombs

ting shot, I stepped off the ramp and thought the water would be ankle deep, but I stepped into a shell crater, so I went down holding all my gear and was completely underwater. The other guys pulled me up, and we started our assault of the cliffs."

The only shelter was at the base of the cliffs. But there, hand grenades and boulders came raining down from above. The one possible route to safety was to begin scaling the cliff face. As the first Rangers started up the ropes, the Germans at the top began cutting them. More than one Ranger would later recall thinking that their mission would not succeed.

Then, more good news: the destroyers U.S.S. *Satterlee* and H.M.S. *Talybont*, seeing the Rangers' plight, drove directly toward shore, unleashing their heavy guns on the cliff line at close range. On the beach below, several Rangers set up mortars and began firing at the German positions above. The naval cannons and mortar fire drove most of the Germans back from the edge of the cliff and allowed the Rangers to resume their ascent. "I've got to get up there," Lomell remembers telling himself. "I've got to get those guns."

Although the men later said the ascent seemed to take an eternity, the first Rangers reached the summit of Pointe du Hoc five minutes after Rudder's LCA landed. Within 15 minutes, more than 200 fighting men were fanning out from the top of the cliffs. The Germans—stunned that anyone had over-

come the natural obstacles of Pointe du Hoc—fell back but kept peppering the Rangers with machine-gun fire. The Americans took shelter in ready-made trenches left by the Allied bombardment.

A heart-breaking moment followed: when the Rangers stormed the gun fortifications and pulled back the camouflage netting, they found telephone poles rather than cannons—the Germans had fooled Allied reconnaissance. This gave rise to a widely circulated myth that the mission at Pointe du Hoc was unnecessary. In fact, although Allied intelligence reports had been wrong about the exact location of the 155-mm guns, they were correct that such guns were present on the cliffs and about the necessity of destroying them.

Searching the concrete bunker, Lomell quickly noticed tracks in the dirt floor leading away from the embrasure. He and a Ranger squad followed the tracks and within minutes found five heavy guns hidden in an apple orchard. Incredibly,

Artifact

Grappling Hook

Expecting the Germans atop Pointe du Hoc would try to cut the ropes they were climbing, the Rangers attached a lighted fuse to the grappling hooks that held the ropes in place, leading the Germans to believe that the hooks were a weapon that was about to explode.

they were unguarded. Using thermite grenades (which don't explode but generate heat intense enough to melt a machine's moving parts), they wrecked the guns—which had been aimed at Utah Beach and were ready to fire. At almost the same moment, another Ranger squad stumbled upon a German ammunition dump and blew it up.

At 0900, less than two hours after stepping ashore, Rudder was able to send the coded message PRAISE THE LORD, signaling to his superior, General Clarence Huebner, that the Rangers had accomplished their mission. But owing to confusion in Allied communications, the message didn't get through to Huebner, who had believed since 0700 (when Rudder's signal flare hadn't appear) that the attack had failed. Meanwhile, by midday, the Germans had organized themselves for the first of what would be several counterattacks. The Rangers held off each of these thrusts but suffered more wounded and killed with each new German foray.

In the late afternoon, Rudder sent another message asking for aid. This one was received by Huebner, who messaged back, NO REINFORCEMENTS AVAILABLE—ALL RANGERS HAVE LANDED AT OMAHA. Surrounded on three sides, with their backs to the cliff, the Rangers held off five onslaughts by ever larger contingents of German troops, through D-day and D-day plus one. They were not relieved until June 8. By that time, only 90 of Rudder's original force of 225 men were able to fight.

In 1954 *Collier's* magazine invited James Rudder and his son to tour Pointe du Hoc on the 10th anniversary of D-day. The former Ranger looked around as if seeing the place for the first time and blurted out, "Will you tell me how we did this? Anybody would be a fool to try this. It was crazy then, and it's crazy now." ∎

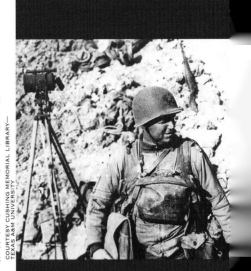

FOR THE RECORD: Six days after D-day, the Rangers re-create their exploits for posterity

Always Climbing Higher

Born into a large family in the West Texas town of Eden, James Earl Rudder worked his father's ranch until leaving to attend Texas A&M University. He graduated in 1932 with a degree in industrial education, a football letter and a second lieutenant's commission in the U.S. Army Reserve.

But there was scant demand for industrial education by 1932, because the Great Depression had insured that there was very little left of American industry. So Rudder took the only work he could find—he dug ditches for several years. In the mid-1930s, he was hired as a high school teacher in the town of Brady (where he would settle for the rest of his life), then was an instructor and football coach at John Tarleton Agricultural College. Along the way, he married Margaret Williamson, a student at the University of Texas.

As war approached, Rudder was called to active duty in June 1941. He came home from World War II with the rank of full colonel and a chestful of medals: the Distinguished Service Cross, Silver Star, Bronze Star, Purple Heart and French Legion of Honor with Croix de Guerre and Palm. He went on to successful careers in business, ranching and politics, serving as mayor of Brady for six years and later as Texas Land Commissioner.

But Rudder is best remembered (apart from his war service) for his tenure as president of Texas A&M University. Taking over in 1959, he shepherded the institution through profound changes, including the admission of women, racial integration and the abolition of compulsory ROTC service, while fostering the higher academic standards that transformed a regional agricultural college into a world-class university. In France, however, Rudder will always be recalled as the liberator of Pointe du Hoc. Every March 23, the residents of the nearby town of Criqueville hold a memorial service to observe the anniversary of his death in 1970.

Sword/Gold Beaches

SITUATION REPORT Omaha Beach A tight spot: the Navy suspends further landings of troops until congestion on the beach can be cleared; Allied destroyers close on the beach to supply fire support to besieged U.S. troops • **Gold Beach** Kampfgruppe Meyer is ordered to counterattack British forces advancing off the beach • **Sword Beach** Commandos attack Ouistreham; British infanty advance on Hermanville • **Juno Beach** Canadian forces advance toward St. Croix-sur-Mer

---

O FF SWORD BEACH AT 0800 HOURS, A RANGY SCOTSMAN who had become a legend at the age of 31 for his bravery in the bungled 1942 raid on Dieppe waited aboard his landing boat, scanning the shore as the craft rocked up and down in the 6-ft. waves, trying to catch a glimpse of how the first groups to land were faring. The Scotsman was Simon Christopher Joseph Fraser, a.k.a. Lord Lovat of Britain's House of Lords, a.k.a. the chieftain of Clan Fraser. Friends took the easy way out; they called him "Simie." A contemporary described Lovat as "a mixture of Davey Crockett and Lafayette"; he was the founder, presiding spirit and leader of the 1st Special Service Brigade, Scottish commandos known for the jaunty green berets they preferred to helmets.

As the landing boats from the first wave made their way back to the transport ships to pick up more troops, Lovat hailed one of them. The craft drew alongside, and Lovat could see that her sides were dented and riddled with holes. Parts of the boat were on fire and it seemed to be in danger of sinking. Some of the crew were dead; others were lying mangled on her decks. Only one man was standing, clinging to the wheel, blood running down his face.

"How was the landing?" Lovat called.

The figure straightened up, lifted his one good arm and made Winston Churchill's V-for-Victory salute. "A piece of cake," he replied.

The remark perfectly captures the landings at Sword and Gold beaches, the two sites assigned to the British by Operation Overlord planners. While far from a piece of cake, the landings at the two beaches proceeded in generally orderly fashion—following a tough first few hours—with far fewer Allied casualties than at Omaha and Juno beaches. More than 50,000 British troops were assigned to land at Sword and Gold (in addition, 9,000 British troops landed with the Canadians at Juno Beach). Gold Beach was at the western end of

SWORD BEACH: Soldiers of the 1st Battalion, South Lancashire Regiment, move onto the beach. Their commander bore the battalion colors onto the beach and was immediately cut down by German machine guns

BRITISH WAR OFFICE

JUNE 6, 1944

"Get down, you mad bastard. You're attracting attention to us!"

—Unknown sergeant, to Scottish bagpiper Bill Millin

LAYING LOW: Early in the fighting, British troops take cover as they wait to move forward off Sword Beach. At both Sword and Gold beaches, the troops moved from the shore into small seaside towns and immediately faced house-to-house combat with dug-in Germans

the three Anglo-Canadian beaches. It was assigned to the British 50th Division, whose goal was to move ashore, take the town of Arromanches—slated to be the site of one of the artificial Mulberry harbors—then occupy the historic town of Bayeux and link up with U.S. forces coming off Omaha Beach.

Sword Beach, the farthest left flank of the Allied landing sites, was assigned to the 3rd Infantry Division. Their mission: to move inland quickly and link up with British paratroopers and glider-borne troops under the command of Major John Howard, who had landed in the area in the early morning hours of June 6. Howard's men were assigned to take and hold the important bridges over the Caen Canal and the Orne River. The units moving off Sword were then supposed to move forward and occupy Caen.

Although the landings went well at both Sword and Gold beaches, the British troops did not achieve their stated prime objective on D-day: to take and hold the critical crossroads town of Caen. The reason lies not with the troops, who performed well, but with their commander, Field Marshal Bernard Montgomery, who simply raised the bar of success too high for his men. The so-called failure of the British to take Caen has overshadowed the very real achievements of British troops on D-day.

Montgomery, perhaps Britain's greatest hero of World War II—and Eisenhower's No. 2 man for Operation Overlord's ground forces—set an impossible goal, for Caen lies eight miles inland from the beaches, and the landings at Sword and Gold were scheduled to provide a slow, steady buildup of troops rather than the sudden massive influx of men and armor needed for such an audacious venture. In fact, the British troops did well to penetrate as far as they did; the most advanced troops dug in for the night some three miles short of Caen, the gateway that guarded the road to Paris. Caen would not fall to Allied hands until the third week of July.

B UT THAT'S GETTING AHEAD OF OUR STORY. IN THEIR LANDing craft bobbing up and down off Sword Beach, Lord Lovat and his commandos in the second landing wave are now drawing near the shore, pockmarked here and there by the strong naval bombardment that began at 0545. The Allied navy that stood off Sword Beach was a floating United Nations that included British, Polish and Norwegian ships. In one of the few naval offensives undertaken by the Germans on D-day, at 0530 a German E-boat operating out of Le Havre torpedoed the destroyer H.M.N.S. *Svenner,* one of 10 Norwegian ships in action; she sank, and 34 of her crew died.

Despite the standard Overlord softening-up—a strong naval bombardment and bombing runs—the Germans managed to direct a good deal of ammunition at Sword Beach. The soldiers in the first wave faced withering fire; the East Yorkshire Regiment suffered 200 casualties in its first minutes ashore. But because of 6-ft. waves, the duplex-drive amphibious tanks had been released closer to Sword than planned, a spur-of-the-moment decision that allowed 21 of 25 of them to reach dry land. These swimming tanks, with a strong assist from the mine-sweeping flailing tanks developed by British General Percy Hobart, helped the Britons secure the beach, and they quickly began moving into the towns along the shore.

Lovat and his men landed at 0820 hours. Among his con-

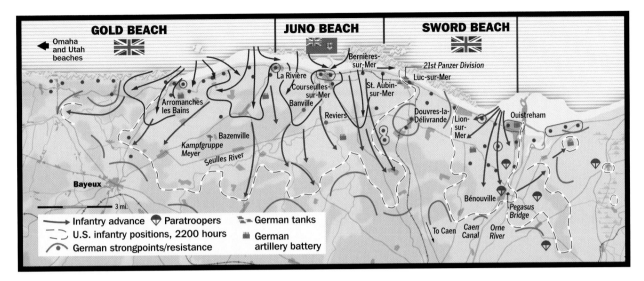

GOLD BEACH

← Omaha
and Utah
beaches

JUNO BEACH

Bernières-
sur-Mer

La Rivière

Courseulles-
sur-Mer

Arromanches
les Bains

Banville

St. Aubin-
sur-Mer

SWORD BEACH

21st Panzer Division

Luc-sur-Mer

Reviers

Douvres-la-
Délivrande

Lion-
sur-
Mer

Ouistreham

Bazenville

Kampfgruppe
Meyer

Seulles River

Bénouville

Pegasus
Bridge

Bayeux

To Caen

Caen
Canal

Orne
River

— 3 mi.

→ Infantry advance   ⊕ Paratroopers   ⊱ German tanks

U.S. infantry positions, 2200 hours   ▥ German
artillery battery

German strongpoints/resistance

tingent were 178 Free French troops, the only French to land on D-day. One of them was combat nurse Gwenn-Ael Bollore, who recalled the landing for TIME in 1994: "As the day started to break we saw France—this tiny little strip of land—appear. It was the most moving moment for me. You're there, in the silence, you see the coast; you know that something terrible is going to happen. The British commander ordered that the French boats should beach, symbolically, a few yards ahead of the others. We appreciated that. We had 550 yds. of bare beach to cross, and nowhere to hide. There were people falling around us."

Scottish commando leader Peter Masters takes up the tale: "Nobody dashed ashore. We staggered. With one hand I car-

ried my gun, finger on the trigger, with the other I held onto the rope-rail down the ramp, and with the third hand I carried my bicycle … Our brigadier, Lord Lovat, was walking about in the forming-up area urging on people. He seemed to be a man perfectly at ease, and shots and the noise in general didn't seem to bother him at all. 'Good show, the piper,' he said to the bagpiper who had piped us ashore as he came dashing up. Lovat walked around in the forming-up area, urging everybody on, saying, 'Come on, get a move on, this is no different than an exercise.' He was very calm. He carried no weapon other than his Colt .45 at his holster. Instead, he had a walking stick." But as bagpiper Bill Millin tells the story, there was at least one person on the beach who didn't care for

MID-MORNING: Commandos (who have traded berets for helmets) race through the streets of Ouistreham. Duplex-drive tanks with canvas "skirts" collapsed offer support

IN THE COUNTRYSIDE: British infantrymen storm a German-held farmhouse, already burning and badly damaged, in this picture from German war archives

his music: "This sergeant came running over and said: 'Get down, you mad bastard. You're attracting attention to us!'"

At the three Anglo-Canadian beaches, the invading forces in many cases moved directly from the shore onto the streets of seaside towns, whose buildings had been carefully fortified by the Germans. As the British advanced off Sword and into the streets of Luc-sur-Mer, they were held up by fierce German resistance: unknown to the landing groups, a unit of the German 21st Panzer Division, under Major General Edgar Feuchtinger, was in the area. The British managed to disable the column of tanks—foiling the Germans' single best chance at driving a wedge between the landing beaches—but the British advance off the beach was delayed. The invaders fared better in Ouistreham, where the Germans holed up in the heavily fortified casino; the British finally took it by mounting an attack from the rear. But the unexpected presence of the 21st Panzer Division—one unit of which took up positions in the streets of Caen—ensured the city would not fall on D-day.

WHILE THE BRITISH WERE MAKING SIGNIFICANT, IF SLOWer than expected, headway at Sword, their counterparts at Gold Beach were also doing well. The landings here were planned an hour later than the U.S. landings at Utah and Omaha, owing to tide conditions, offering the gunners aboard the Royal Navy ships offshore an extra 60 minutes to pound the German positions. As a result, the most damage to the troops coming ashore at Gold was caused by the heavily mined barricades placed along the surf and shore. The "hedgehogs" and other barriers not only claimed lives and boats; they also took up precious time, as frogmen, sappers and tank crews fought to take them out of action.

As at Sword, the delays on the beach pointed out just how

unrealistic Montgomery's goals had been: he had assigned the Gold invaders to take Bayeux by day's end. But a German regiment, Kampfgruppe Meyer, put up a stand at Bazenville, outside Bayeux, and stopped the advance of the British 50th Division. The capture of Bayeux would have to wait until D-day plus one. But important goals were won at Gold, including the taking of Arromanches, slated to be the site of one of the giant artificial Mulberry harbors. And a huge British force was now ashore: more than 28,000 men landed at Sword Beach on D-day and 25,000 more at Gold Beach.

Meanwhile, Lord Lovat and his green berets were late for a very important date: Lovat had promised Major John Howard of the British 6th Airborne Division that he would link up with Howard's paratroopers and glider-borne troops at the bridges over the River Orne and the Caen Canal at 1215 hours. Howard kept his part of the bargain; his brilliant surprise at-

Artifact

Folding Bicycle

Both British and Canadian troops brought folding bikes with them on June 6, to the derision of U.S. forces. One American officer brought a bike aboard his landing craft, only to have it thrown overboard mid-Channel.

tack from the air wrested both objectives from the Germans just after midnight.

As the morning wore on, the beleaguered paratroopers, under merciless enemy pressure, began to steal glum looks at their watches. At 1214 a weary officer muttered, "They'll never make it now." At that moment, through the crash and rattle of gunfire and mortar shells, came a distant skirling of bagpipes. A paratrooper bugler answered with the call of *Defaulters*, indicating that the road immediately ahead had Germans on it, and that the first commandos should go around them.

At exactly 1217:30 a tall, slim officer with a rifle slung over one shoulder scrambled up the bank of the Caen Canal. Behind Lord Lovat came piper Billy Millin, and behind the piper a long line of green-bereted commandos. Brigadier Nigel Poett, commander of the 5th Parachute Brigade, came up to shake Lord Lovat's hand. Their greeting was brief—and British.

Poett: "We are really most pleased to see you."

Lovat: "Thank you. Sorry we were two and a half minutes late."

WELL, THAT'S THE WAY TIME PRINTED THE STORY IN 1944, AS DID HUNDREDS of newspapers around the world; the classically understated greeting of the two British officers became part of the legend and lore of the invasion. After the war, Lord Lovat, a stickler for honesty, claimed that the encounter was slightly less memorable: He told an American magazine reporter in 1945 that, while he wished the encounter had been quite so memorable, it was actually rather hackneyed. What really happened, Lovat said, was that Poett stepped up to him and quoted African explorer Henry Stanley: "Doctor Livingstone, I presume?"

American D-day expert Stephen Ambrose also quibbles with the classic account of the meeting at the bridge: he places its time at 1300 hours and says other commandos, not Lovat, were the first to greet the paratroopers. But it's the fact of the linkup, not its exacting timing (or wording) that matters. John Ford, the great Hollywood director, was present at D-day, shooting documentary footage of the invasion for the U.S. Army. In his 1962 film, *The Man Who Shot Liberty Valance*, Ford has James Stewart argue for the importance of myth-making: "When the legend becomes fact, print the legend." We've decided to print both versions of the linkup between the British forces, so readers can take their choice. ∎

SIGN LANGUAGE: When British troops took the Hindenburg Bastion, a major German emplacement, they renamed it, with a nod to British General Charles Orde Wingate's "chindits," a guerrilla group in Burma

Lovat's Green Berets

When Simon Fraser, Lord Lovat, led his commandos across the Channel, he was tracing his family history in reverse: the first Fraser departed Normandy in 1066 and landed in England with William the Conqueror. Since that time, Clan Fraser and its chieftain have been a force to reckon with: the 11th Lord Lovat fought with the Scots at Culloden in 1746, was captured and tried by the English and became the last aristocrat to be beheaded in England.

His modern descendant pushed for the creation of a British commando unit before the war; he succeeded and led the training, turning his green berets into guerrilla fighters with a harsh regimen in the Scottish highlands. The oddball cast of teachers included saboteurs from occupied Europe, elderly dons from the science labs of Oxford, Arctic explorers, second-story men on leave from British jails and former Shanghai policemen. But a 1945 *Cosmopolitan* article on Lovat's school that claimed, "One instructor actually bicycled 500 miles to the training center living on nothing but lawn-mowings," was, perhaps, exaggerated.

The training paid off in a series of successful raids in Norway early in the war. At Dieppe in 1942, Lovat's men provided one of the failed raid's few high points when they put a six-gun German battery out of action. Lovat's D-day exploits became legend, although he later quibbled with the account of his linkup with the paratroopers. Six days after D-day, Lovat was badly wounded by a German shell, was given a transfusion on the battlefield, then spent months recuperating in Scotland; his war was over. Lovat died in 1995, one year after both his oldest and youngest sons died unexpectedly.

JUNE 6, 1944

"We'll start the war right here."

—Attributed to Brigadier General Theodore Roosevelt Jr.

Utah Beach

SITUATION REPORT Omaha Beach Two German fortifications, WN60 and WN70, fall to the slowly advancing American troops ● **Sword Beach** Three vehicle exits are cleared; commandos subdue the Riva Bella Casino strongpoint ● **Juno Beach** Despite sustaining horrific losses while landing, surviving Allied invaders regroup and rally, attacking the Langrune strongpoint. Canadian and British forces advance inland and begin to subdue the towns of Courseulles and Bernières

U.S. ARMY SIGNAL CORPS

ACHING WITH ARTHRITIS—AND BEARING THE SCARS of two wounds from World War I—the oldest U.S. fighting man in the entire invasion force brandished a walking stick and bore a .45 strapped to his shoulder as he hobbled ashore from his landing boat on Utah Beach. He was the first U.S. general to come ashore on D-day, and he wore no helmet; he scorned them. Instead, he wore an old cap. By this time, amphibious landings themselves were old hat to the 57-year-old, for Normandy was his third of the war—he had landed in the first waves at Oran in North Africa and at Gela in Sicily. Thousands of G.I.s knew his cocky figure and the wide-mouthed grin on his battered face. When he marched in review on ceremonial occasions, soldiers' spines starched up and the divisional band burst into *Old Soldiers Never Die*. He favored the troops in the front lines, and they loved him back, uplifted by his gallant, gamecock spirit. His name was pretty easy to remember too: Theodore Roosevelt Jr.

Teddy Roosevelt's namesake and oldest son wasn't just the first general ashore on D-day: he may have been on the very first Allied craft to hit the beach that morning—an honor that surely would have pleased him, if he had had time to appreciate it. For when Roosevelt came ashore around 0610, he didn't know where the hell he was. However, he did know where he wasn't—at his carefully planned landing site.

At Utah beach—in stark contrast to Omaha—the first three components of the four-part invasion strategy worked well on June 6. While the Allied invaders waited offshore to land, their paratrooper colleagues had worked through the night to secure key positions inland of Utah. Then, at 0550, U.S. Navy ships began delivering shells inland, and the effort was amplified within minutes by a bombing run of 270 Martin Marauder medium bombers. Though most German bunkers and other gun emplacements survived the double blow, the men who manned the positions—a ragtag group heavy on captured

MOVE OUT! By 0940 on D-day morning, Colonel James Van Fleet could report to higher-ups: "I am ashore with Colonel Simmons and General Roosevelt, advancing steadily." Most Allied objectives were achieved at Utah

IN CHARGE: Dug in and awaiting orders to move inland, troops protect the enormous stores of arms and equipment now steadily coming ashore at Utah Beach

Russian "volunteers" and older, feeble "white bread" German units—were seriously shaken. They put up little resistance as the first wave of troops hit the shore.

But the fourth component at Utah, the landing itself, went seriously off-kilter: Roosevelt and the other troops in the first wave landed a full kilometer, almost two-thirds of a mile, south of their designated zone. What went wrong? Three of the four LCCs (Landing Craft Control) serving as guides for the

first wave hit German mines and went out of action long before reaching their designated target areas. Without these floating navigational directors, many of the boats carrying troops ashore lost their bearings. And a wind-churned current that was running strongly north to south at Utah carried the landing boats well off their path.

But luck was with the Americans: the navigational miscue turned out to be a blessing in disguise. If the men had landed at their intended target, they would have been smack-dab in the middle of a potent German position, defended by tough obstacles on the beach and a tougher gun emplacement above. But the eastern portion of Utah Beach was lightly defended.

As a bewildered Roosevelt studied his map and scanned the horizon for landmarks, he noticed a windmill that gave him his bearings. More important, he realized that the first troops ashore were facing little opposition from the Germans. When Colonel James Van Fleet, CO of the 8th Regiment, 4th Division, came ashore, the two men huddled and made an on-the-spot call: rather than attempt to follow their orders and relocate their efforts to the planned target site, they would set up their beachhead here, instruct other landing craft to follow their lead, then begin sending their troops inland. "We'll start the war right here," Roosevelt is supposed to have declared (the remark may be apocryphal). The can-do decision exem-

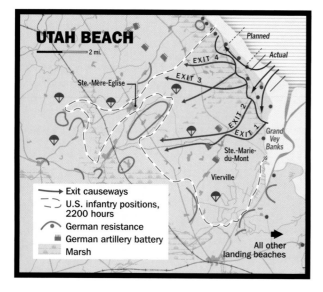

UTAH BEACH

|— 2 mi. —|

Planned
Actual

EXIT 4
EXIT 3
EXIT 2
EXIT 1

Ste.-Mère-Eglise

Grand
Vey
Banks

Ste.-Marie-du-Mont

Vierville

→ Exit causeways
⌐⌐ U.S. infantry positions, 2200 hours
⌒ German resistance
🏭 German artillery battery
░ Marsh

→ All other landing beaches

plified the sort of individual initiative—unimaginable in the German ranks—that would help win the day for the Allies.

Harper Coleman, also of the 8th Regiment, recalled the scene in Gerald Astor's *June 6, 1944: The Voices of D-Day:* "When we came ashore, we had a greeter. How he got there I do not know, except that he was in one of the first landing craft. But Brigadier General Roosevelt was standing there, waving his cane and giving out instructions as only he could. If we were afraid of the enemy, we were more afraid of him and could not have stopped on the beach had we wanted."

THANKS TO THE QUICK THINKING OF ROOSEVELT AND VAN FLEET, UTAH TURNED out to be the least costly beach the Allies won on D-day: the total number of dead, wounded and missing was fewer than 200. Others also improvised off the scenario envisioned by Overlord's planners so long before. Heads-up Navy skippers launched the swimming duplex-drive Sherman tanks closer to shore than called for in the plan: of 32 tanks, 28 made it ashore—though a bit after the first wave of troops—and provided strong cover for the men. Engineering units worked efficiently to create large gaps in the beach barriers, then blasted avenues through the seawall for the steady waves of tanks, trucks and machinery that were arriving ashore.

Indeed, as Roosevelt, Van Fleet and others continued moving men off the beach, the biggest problem of the morning turned out to be sheer congestion. Utah turned into a traffic jam, and a potentially deadly one: many enemy mines still had not been defused. Adding to the confusion was the increasing number of soldiers on the German side who were surrendering. But the U.S. soldiers kept pushing, and before noon the traffic jam had moved off the beach and onto the four major causeways—"exits" in Overlord lingo—that led inland, the key objectives of the Utah landing.

The Germans had flooded the low-lying fields around the causeways, intending to confine invaders to these narrow avenues where they could be isolat-

Chip off the Old Block

When the first Roosevelts lived in the White House," TIME wrote in its July 24, 1944, issue, "not even the most delicately carved period chair was safe during leap-frog sessions … Teddy's four sons and two daughters roller skated on the shiny hardwood floors, burrowed through attics and ceilings, wobbled all over the White House on stilts … This was the era of the Strenuous Life, and the Roosevelt children lived it.

"World War I changed strenuous living from pranks to patriotism. Quentin, the ex-President's youngest son, was killed at the age of 20 in an air battle with two German planes … Kermit came through unhurt; Archie was badly wounded; Theodore Jr. , the oldest, was gassed once, wounded twice and decorated 15 times. All three surviving brothers joined up again in World War II. Kermit died, at 53, on active duty in Alaska in June 1943. Archie, wounded last month, at 50 is a lieutenant colonel, fighting on Biak Island. 'Young Teddy' saw action in Tunisia, Sicily, Italy and Normandy, was thrice wounded."

Teddy Jr. spent the first half of his life overshadowed by his father, and most of the last half overshadowed by his fifth cousin, Franklin. Following his father's path, Teddy Jr. transformed himself from sickly kid to robust youngster, then moved from Harvard University to the New York State Legislature to Assistant Secretary of the Navy. He ran for the governorship of New York State in 1924 but lost to Al Smith. He later served as Governor of both Puerto Rico and the Philippines.

In the 1936 campaign, loyal Republican Teddy Jr. called Franklin Roosevelt "my fifth cousin about-to-be removed." Yet after Pearl Harbor, he briskly admonished an interviewer: "Remember, it's our country, our war and our President." He was activated for Army duty in 1942.

Artifact

Utah Beach Diary

Lieut. Sidney J. Montz of the 8th Infantry Regiment, 4th Infantry Division, kept this diary at Utah Beach, in which he notes the confidence instilled by General Roosevelt as well as the botched landing location, well south of the target site.

> time to move or they will kill us all. Gen Roosevelt gave me lots of courage. Co."A" about 500yds. to front finally got over with Wittenberger + one section, Another Sec. coming up. Under small arms + artillery fire. Navy left us 1000 yds. too far
>
> left, the left outfit caught hell. Moved in very fast, every house + tree loaded with men, they fire at you from all directions, very hard to see them as they use smokeless powder. Will get on to them soon then they will catch hell

ed and devastated. That wasn't a problem on Exit 1, the causeway heading southwest off the beach: around 1100 hours, U.S. troops advancing on the far end of a causeway were delighted to discover that it was held not by Germans but by Americans. Paratroopers of the 101st Airborne Division had landed during the night and succeeded in capturing the small town of Pouppeville. This was the first meeting on D-day between the troops who parachuted into France and the troops who landed from the sea.

On the exits leading northwest off the beach, U.S. commanders again defied their orders, improvised and carried the day. Held back by a traffic jam on the Exit 4 causeway, Colonel Russell (Red) Reeder, commanding the 12th Infantry Division, abandoned it and led his men on a soggy detour through adjacent flooded meadows; after two or three hours, they emerged on the high ground, close to their assigned destination for the day, outside the towns of St. Martin and St. Germain. Here they linked up with U.S. paratroopers from the 82nd Airborne Division.

By nightfall, some 23,500 troops and 1,700 vehicles had landed on Utah Beach. Teddy Roosevelt Jr. could be proud of his work that day, but he was not given time to savor the victory. On June 9, he suffered a heart attack while in his jeep, "Rough Rider"; he died three days later. The Medal of Honor he received for his "gallantry and intrepidity" at Utah Beach was awarded posthumously. ∎

1000-1100 Hours

Juno Beach

SITUATION REPORT **Omaha Beach** The order is given to resume landings, but it cannot be carried out immediately because of congestion in sealanes approaching the beach ● **Gold Beach** La Rivière Lighthouse falls to advancing British troops ● **Sword Beach** British tank forces begin the drive toward Caen. Germans begin counterattack toward Lion-sur-Mer, where they will meet tough resistance ● **Utah Beach** Movement inland continues despite congestion on key causeways

ALL ASHORE! Later on D-day, with Juno Beach fully in Allied hands, troops of the 9th Canadian Infantry Brigade—bicycles in hand—pour into the town of Bernières-sur-Mer, where the high tides are almost up to the seawall. The placid scene belies the deadly fighting earlier in the day; the houses at left were damaged in the bombardment

RECALLING THE CHANNEL CROSSING OF HIS CANADIAN division for Time in 1994, Dan Darling said: "Going over, the officers read a message from Ike. One of the guys prayed and then joked that this time he really meant it [the prayer]." Darling, who went ashore at Juno Beach, continued, "The first sight of France was the smoke, then the fires on the beach. There was so much happening: shells whistling in, buildings burning, aircraft overhead, Jerry letting go with 88-mm guns. We all grabbed our bicycles, and I remember the water under my chin. I had 78 lbs. of gear, not counting the bike and steel helmet. There were bodies in the water, and bodies lined up under blankets on the shore."

Darling and his fellow Canadians—15,000 of them, supported by 9,000 British troops—were out for revenge. At Juno, it was served cold: the Canadians fought in the memory of their fellow countrymen, who had landed at the French port of Dieppe on Aug. 19, 1942. That mission had been an utter debacle. Dieppe was a key harbor, offering huge advantages to the German defenders, who protected it with strong fortifications and obstacles. In contrast to Overlord's careful planning, the raid on Dieppe was premature and poorly orchestrated. The results were ghastly: of the 6,000 troops in the action, more than 4,000 were killed, wounded or taken prisoner. Seven battalion commanders went in; seven battalion commanders died. It was Canada's greatest tragedy of the war, and Darling and his mates weren't about to forget it.

By day's end, the Canadians would have their revenge. A significant force of men, vehicles and arms landed at Juno on June 6, and Canadian troops penetrated farther inland than any other Allies; one tank unit was among the few units in the entire invasion to achieve its D-day objective. But in the first two hours of the landings, Juno Beach became a killing field that was

JUNE 6, 1944

"You couldn't think about getting killed: either you got them or they got you."

—Dan Darling, shot three times on D-day

THE PUBLIC ARCHIVES OF CANADA

0830: Soldiers come ashore at Juno Beach, where the rough seas that delayed the landing are evident. The soldier at the bottom of the ramp is carrying a Wellbike, a small 2-stroke motorcycle that weighed 70 lbs.

almost as deadly as Omaha Beach.

Waiting in the landing craft, Darling and the troops going in didn't anticipate the hail of fire that would greet them on Juno Beach. A huge midnight bombing by the Royal Canadian Air Force had been followed at dawn by a strike by U.S. B-17s. At 0600, 13 ships of the Royal Navy, joined by Canadian destroyers H.M.C.S. *Algonquin* and *Sioux* and the Free French F.F.S. *Combattante,* unleashed a massive bombardment on the shore. While the bombing runs proved just as ineffective at Juno as they did at most other beaches, the naval guns found their targets. The shelling from offshore didn't put the major German emplacements (*Widerstandnester,* "resistance nests") out of action, but it badly shook up the defenders.

The objectives at Juno were to take the towns along the beach, St. Aubin, Bernières and Courseulles (the most heavily defended of the three), as well as neighboring villages inland, then move toward Caen, where troops were to link up with the British, moving in from Sword and Gold beaches.

The waters off Juno Beach were choppy and treacherous at 0735, when the first landing boats were scheduled to hit the shore. The seas were so rough the landing was delayed by 30 minutes. As a result, many of the mined obstacles slated to be defused while still above water were submerged by the rising tide, and 90 of 306 landing boats were lost, most of them victims of German Teller mines. The choppy waters also claimed eight duplex-drive tanks in the first invasion wave. Many LCT (Landing Craft Tank) skippers watched a few tanks sink and then, defying their orders, landed their tanks right on the beach, where they could support the landing troops.

Once ashore, the men came under enfilading fire (directed from the side) from the German guns, which were mounted to command the beaches from the flanks. The death toll in the first wave was very high; official figures show 1 in 19 men died at Juno on D-day, 1 in 18 at Omaha. But the waves of Canadians kept coming, and they brought their own sound track to the front. As soldiers, engineers and medics jumped into the waves, waded and crawled ashore under fire, then ducked behind tanks to avoid the strafing German guns, the skirling sound of bagpipes urged them on: the Canadian Scottish Regiment was piping away from boats offshore.

The heads-up decision to land many tanks on the beach began making a difference at Juno. And "Hobart's Funnies"—the specialized tanks built by British genius Percy Hobart—also made a significant contribution. Some U.S. commanders had jeered at the specially adapted tanks before the invasion, but at Juno they proved their worth. Flailing tanks with rotating chains in front cleared minefields; flame-throwing tanks cleared out pillboxes. Even the most widely derided of the "Funnies" proved invaluable; in one instance, a Sherman tank bearing a bundle of fascines dropped them into an anti-tank ditch, then itself sank into a huge adjoining crater. Two tanks bearing bridges used the sunken tank as a support and laid a bridge across the chasm; soon men and heavy equipment were crossing the ditch and moving quickly ahead.

In the landings at Juno, like those at Sword and Gold beaches, the invaders moved directly off the shore and into small seaside towns. The nature of the fighting quickly changed from an amphibious beach assault to urban, house-to-house warfare. Germans held fortified positions in the towns, and snipers, machine-gun nests and other emplacements took a heavy toll on the Canadians and British before the sheer weight of the armor coming off the beach began to drive the Germans out of their positions. The fighting in the town of Courseulles was particularly bloody.

BY 1000 HOURS ON D-DAY, THE ALLIES CONTROLLED MOST of the Juno beaches. Sappers were busily defusing mines; supply masters were moving men and equipment ashore in good order. The front was moving through the towns, in some cases meeting tough resistance, in others almost none. By 1200 hours the entire Canadian 3rd Division was ashore, and many units had passed through the towns and into the countryside, which was free of the hedgerows that would keep units bottled up at other landing beaches.

"On the beach," Dan Darling recalled, "there was no standing around. We tried using the fold-up bikes we'd trained on for two years. But the rubble on the roads made the whole thing impractical. After about three miles, we were ordered to stack them up in a heap. We dug slit trenches the first night in a churchyard; Jerry was maybe 1,000 yds. away. When we tried to negotiate with a local farmer to buy some eggs, he was mystified by our Quebec French and finally asked in English 'What do you want?' He had been a steward on the French

Artifact

Counterfeit Franc

Invading soldiers were given counterfeit French francs to spend, over the objections of Charles de Gaulle, who felt the plan devalued France's currency. The bills were printed in both the U.S. and Britain. Most troops were given between $10 and $25 worth of francs.

liner *Normandie* and lived for years in New York. He gave us 15 eggs and green onions, so we made an omelet. Once we got inland, Jerry turned out to be mostly fanatical Hitler Youth and conscripts from Italy, Poland and Austria. The one who shot me [Darling took three bullets in the abdomen] was so young he'd never needed to shave. You couldn't think about getting killed: either you got them, or they got you."

By day's end, the Allies had landed some 21,400 men and 3,200 vehicles at Juno and moved deep inland. The death toll was 335, far lower than had been anticipated. It was a good show for the Brits and Canadians. A story told by Jean Houel, a resident of Courseulles, reminds us of a final, touching aspect of the Juno landings. Recalling D-day for journalist Dan Van Der Vat, he said, "At 7 a.m., there they were … When I went out suddenly I saw a tall fellow in front of me with a typically English helmet, and I said [in English]: 'Here they are, the Tommies!' and the young man answered in French: *'Je suis Canadien.'*" The ghosts of Dieppe had been buried; France's children had come to the aid of their motherland. ∎

RUBBLE: Allied troops take cover behind a shattered barrilcade of logs as they are harassed by a German sniper in the streets of St. Aubin

"They're right in there, giving morphine and bandaging wounds while the bullets whiz past their ears."
—Unknown soldier, quoted in LIFE

The Medics

SITUATION REPORT **Omaha Beach** Landings resume, as two LSTs force their way through approach lanes previously blocked by disabled vehicles • **Juno Beach** The Canadian 9th Brigade lands immediately behind the 8th, causing confusion and overcrowding • **The Enemy** A newly assembled German battle group is moving toward the British position on Gold Beach

FIRST AID: Medics treat a wounded soldier on D-day; the location is not known

U.S. ARMY SIGNAL CORPS

ACCORDING TO AN EXPERT AUTHORITY—GENERAL Omar Bradley—every man who set foot on Omaha Beach on D-day was a hero. Few would disagree. But in the hierarchy of heroism, most invasion veterans award the highest honors to those who came to the beaches unarmed: the Army and Navy combat medics. Late on the morning of June 6—especially at Omaha—these brave men found themselves utterly overwhelmed by the carnage that surrounded them. Elaborate plans had been drawn up for the care of the wounded, calling for fast treatment on the scene, rapid evacuation from the front lines and immediate shipment back to England aboard special hospital ships. Those plans—along with just about everything else on the beaches that morning—were soon blown to smithereens. But that didn't stop the medics from their healing rounds.

Staff Sergeant Alfred Eigenberg, a medic attached to an engineering brigade, told D-day chronicler Cornelius Ryan that in the first hours on Omaha there were so many men wounded that he didn't know "where to start or with whom." There was "a terrible politeness among the more seriously wounded," he recalled. Finding one soldier with his leg laid open from the knee to the pelvis, Eigenberg gave him a shot of morphine, then closed the wound with safety pins.

In the chaos of the landing, the medics, like everyone else, were lucky to get ashore in the right place, much less keep their medical kits intact. Medical units landed in the wrong places, at the wrong times, and often crawled onto the beaches empty-handed. Of 12 surgical teams slated to land on Omaha Beach, only eight made it ashore. With no bases to work from and no surgical equipment at hand, the surgeons immediately went to work, giving rudimentary first aid to the wounded.

Here there were no hospitals, no ambulances, no safe medical havens behind the lines. As historian Stephen Ambrose observed, "The situation was so bad that the evacuation of the wounded was toward the enemy. This may have been unique in military history. The few aid posts that had been set up were at the shingle seawall. Medics took great risks to drag the wounded from the beach to the aid posts. There was little that could be done for them beyond bandaging, splinting, giving morphine and plasma (if the medics had any supplies)."

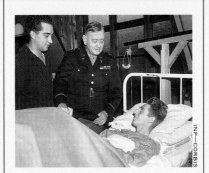

Healer in Chief

When a TIME writer caught up with Major General Paul Ramsey Hawley a few days after D-day, the U.S. Army's top doctor was "pacing the docks at a south-of-England port" [tight military censorship forbade mentioning the town]. Hawley, said TIME, was "making sure for himself that the wounded were comfortable. He saw how tenderly the litter bearers (many of them Negroes) moved the stretchers from ships to docks, from docks to ambulances, watched the doctors change bandages and give morphine in the open air. He sighed with relief: 'Didn't see a single man in pain. Not drugged, mind you—they were smoking cigarettes, many of them—but enough [morphine] so they were comfortable.' Said he when someone asked him how he got such a complicated organization working so smoothly: 'Give a mouse a shot of hooch and he'll yell, 'Bring on the cats.'"

The colorful Hawley later worked with a World War II deputy, Dr. Michael E. DeBakey, to develop the Army's first Mobile Auxiliary Surgical Hospitals. These MASH units were put into service in the Korean conflict, where they are credited with saving hundreds of lives.

Combat medic Jack Fox, who landed at Utah Beach, told British journalist Dan van der Vat, "By the grace of God, I made it ashore and started running through the deep sand toward the seawall. I had saved my medical equipment and stopped to help a wounded soldier lying on the beach. I turned him over and realized he was dead. I recognized him as a friend of mine. I was shocked, scared and angry at the same time." Numerous eyewitnesses say the Germans fired directly at medical corpsmen that morning, in strict violation of the laws of engagement. In fairness, in the chaos of the first hours of the landing, it may have been difficult to distinguish between armed combatants and unarmed medics.

Nor were the medics confined to the beaches. Lieutenant Briand Beaudin, a surgeon who jumped into Normandy as a paratrooper, was taken prisoner; he and other wounded Americans were taken to a German medical center, where he pitched in to help doctors treat injured men from both sides. Beaudin shared medical tips with his enemies, whom he found to be honorable and collegial.

THE MEDICAL CORPS ON D-DAY WAS COMMANDED BY Major General Paul Ramsey Hawley, the Army Surgeon General. Between Pearl Harbor and Overlord, while General George Marshall was rapidly creating a U.S.

HURRY! Well after D-day, Robert Capa took this photo of a U.S. medical convoy moving the wounded in Normandy. By then a complex chain of field hospitals offered quick treatment to the wounded

Army seemingly from scratch, General Hawley was building his own medical army from the ground up. Over three years of intense warfare, Hawley and his team, in constant communication with medics on the front lines, learned a great deal about battlefield medicine, which had made enormous strides in the two decades between World Wars I and II. The development of the new antibiotic "wonder drug," penicillin, along with a new anaesthetic, sodium pentothal, saved thousands of lives. On the home front, where manufacturing had been geared up to a frantic pitch to make America the arsenal of democracy, the U.S. was now also the pharmacy of democracy: some 100 million units of penicillin were produced in the

month before D-day alone. Result: postwar Army statistics showed that fewer than 1% of the wounded men who reached medical stations subsequently died.

Even with the new drugs, Hawley and his team concluded that chemotherapy was no substitute for fast evacuation and prompt surgery. So they recruited surgeons, organized them for front-line work, then trained legions of medical corpsmen, litter bearers, nurses, ambulance drivers and aircraft crews in expediting the wounded. Their mantra, in short: Patch 'em up fast; ship 'em out fast; heal them at leisure.

Hawley created a complex chain of aid stations in the drive for ever faster evacuation. There could be no fixed hospitals

ON THE JOB: Two American nurses, Vaughan Fisher and Margaret Hail, fold dressings in a hospital a few miles behind the front lines. They landed on the beaches on June 10 and walked five miles to this medical station. There were 4,644 U.S. Army nurses stationed on the European front in 1944

BOB LANDRY—TIME LIFE PICTURES

ROBERT HUNT LIBRARY

SUPPLY LINE: Containers of blood for transfusion are lined up at an airfield in Normandy a few days after D-day, just offloaded from a U.S. Army plane. The ETO acronym stands for European Theater of Operations

on the beaches on D-day, but medical ships were part of the vast armada, and many of those wounded on a Normandy beach in the morning found themselves in an Allied hospital in England that very night, or at least aboard a hospital ship. Joe B. Williams was a carpenter's mate aboard the U.S.S. *Bayfield*, a medical craft off Utah Beach, where, he recalled, "there were wounded everywhere—in sick bay, in the mess hall and in the passageways—you couldn't walk anywhere."

By June 10, D-day plus four, the first Allied evacuation hospitals, operating out of tents, had been set up five miles behind the front lines in Normandy. Between July 3 and 18, the 91st Evacuation Hospital cared for 2,549 patients under constant enemy artillery fire. Conditions improved when the artificial Mulberry harbors were completed: entire prefabricated field hospitals were disgorged onto the piers, carried inland on trucks and assembled behind the lines.

At the far end of the chain of healing was England. A LIFE reporter who visited the docks on the evening of June 7 recorded the scene: "Invasion reporters who never got to France at all found a minor epic in the return of the wounded to English ports on the day after the first assault. Some of them walked off the ships, with their uniforms torn and their bandages hastily applied, but swiftly and safely carried out of the battle zone. Others came on stretchers carried by Negro litter bearers, their personal belongings piled beside them. Some carried their boots, with French sand still clinging to the soles, on their litters. Many spoke of fine work done by medical men on the beaches. Said one man: 'They're right in there, giving morphine and bandaging wounds while the bullets whiz past their ears.' Another report told of a difficult abdominal operation performed in a pitching LST under improvised lights.

"Three wounded Canadians chose an unorthodox but astonishingly simple method of getting themselves to a hospital in England...they walked out of a dockyard to which they had been brought and hailed a taxi. Their leader, Lieutenant C.R. Bond of the Royal Canadian Navy, said to hospital attendants: 'We're back from France.'" ∎

Artifact

Utility Belt

Navy Corpsman Leo Scheer's landing craft sank under him at Omaha Beach. He swam ashore wearing the belt at right, which still holds a few bandages. "We lost all our medical supplies," he recalled, "and were forced to take the bandages from the dead to use on the living. The belt is dear to me because the bandages came from the G.I.s who gave up their lives at Omaha Beach."

1200-1300 Hours

The Engineers

SITUATION REPORT Omaha Beach The first American forces to move inland are assaulting the village of Coleville • **Juno Beach** The entire Canadian 3rd Division has come ashore, and elements of the group have managed to penetrate more than a mile inland, capturing several significant bridges over the River Seulles

"FIRE IN THE HOLE!" THROUGHOUT D-DAY MORNING, amid the sound and fury on every landing beach, the cry went up again and again, as some of the toughest men of the Allied force went about their work: destroying the immense barriers of steel, concrete and wire the Germans had placed in their path. U.S. Navy sailors called these combat demolition engineers "Seabees," for Construction Battalions, their original assignment; British troops called them "sappers." Most D-day veterans call them heroes: they took on one of the day's ugliest challenges, saved countless lives and played a critical role in Operation Overlord's success.

At Omaha Beach, even though every one of 16 demolition teams landed off-target, and some washed up onshore minus their explosives, the take-charge engineers managed to create five or six gaps in the obstacles along the beach.

At Utah Beach, Seabees were assigned to the first barriers, the submerged obstacles. Seabee Orval Wakefield, in an oral history on file at the Eisenhower Center at the University of New Orleans, recounts their success: "When we first came in there was nothing there but men running, turning and dodging. All of a sudden it was like a beehive. Boats were able to come in through the obstacles. Bulldozers were pushing sand up against the seawall and half-tracks and tanks were able to go into the interior. It looked like an

PREFAB PIERS: "Port Winston," the Mulberry harbor off Arromanches, takes shape. Beneath the waves, giant concrete caissons connect the sunken ships that act as breakwaters for the enormous artificial creation

"Piers for use on beaches. They must float up and down with tide ... Let me have the best solution worked out. Don't argue the matter. The difficulties will argue for themselves."—Winston Churchill

anthill." The breakthrough was thanks to Wakefield and his comrades, who watched as Army demolition engineers went on to blow up the next set of obstacles, on the beach itself. Next stop: the seawall further up the beach, again breached by Army tanks fitted with bulldozer blades.

These front-line combat engineers played a vital role in the success of the landings. But the fingerprints of engineers were all over Overlord, from the undersea pipeline that delivered oil to Allied vehicles in France to the strategic breakthrough that made the invasion possible in the first place: the artificial harbors that would land the vast supplies needed to sustain Allied momentum once the beachheads were won.

World War II was a machine-age war: it harnessed mass production to violence and transformed Henry Ford's assembly line workers from carmakers into bomber builders. Racing to become Franklin Roosevelt's "arsenal of democracy," the entire U.S. home front hummed in synch to factory whistles, as workers—many of them women—built the machines that won the war. Indeed, Operation Overlord was itself a kind of gigantic mechanism, timed down to the second, relying on the meshing of thousands of complex gears to succeed. All too often those gears failed to mesh, but the planners of Overlord had built so much duplication into their plan that the invasion succeeded despite a host of snafus.

ROLLING: By July, Allied drivers could head straight onto shore on the sturdy surface of a Mulberry artificial harbor

Engineers first breathed life into Overlord. The Germans knew that a major invasion would demand the constant replenishment of men and matériel. Experience told them that the Allies would have to land either at or near a major port city, an artery where quartermasters could offload the supplies that would keep the the invasion's heart pumping. The 1942 calamity at Dieppe convinced the Germans that by fortifying the major French ports, they could repel a landing.

So the Allies thought around the obstacle, much as Hitler's generals, in the first flush of German victories four years before, had bypassed the vaunted Maginot Line. It was—no surprise—Winston Churchill who came up with the notion of creating artificial ports. In a May 30, 1942, memo, he wrote to Admiral Lord Louis Mountbatten of the Royal Navy: "Piers for use on beaches. They must float up and down with tide. The anchor problem must be mastered. Let me have the best solution worked out. Don't argue the matter. The difficulties will argue for themselves." It was a liberating challenge, one that could make Overlord feasible, but only if the Prime Minister's "difficulties" could be solved.

Two Britons solved them. J.D. Bernal, a brilliant (and Marxist) Camridge professor, wowed Churchill with his plans for prefabricated harbors by demonstrating them with paper boats in a bathtub aboard the *Queen Mary*. Brigadier Bruce White refined Bernal's ideas at the Kingswood School in Bath, England, where a mulberry tree was a noted feature of the cam-

JUNE 16: A team of military engineers uses inflatable rafts to build a pontoon bridge across a stream outside the village of St. Sauveur le Vicomte

JUNE 13: As Allied troops move inland, medics offer first aid to a combat engineer who was injured when he stepped on a mine. Another engineer seeks more mines; the Germans placed millions of them in Normandy

pus; the code word for the artificial-port plan became Mulberry. Essential to its success was the sinking of 60-some aging ships to serve as breakwaters; they became "Gooseberries."

A work force of 20,000 men labored for eight months and used 2 million tons of concrete and steel to build the 200 huge segments, or caissons, that were the spine for the two harbors, each of which would enclose more than two square miles of water. Simply hauling the enormous caissons across the Channel required the work of every tugboat in England, with a little help from U.S. tugs.

By D-day's end, Commander Rupert Curtis of the 200th Flotilla, a fleet of landing craft, could report, as he stood off Sword Beach: "Already parts of the prefabricated Mulberry harbors were under tow from England to be placed in position off Arromanches." Incredibly, the harbors began seeing

Artifact

A typical kit used by a combat demolition engineer on D-day would have included plastic explosives, blasting caps and wire to connect the charge to the plunger at top. Once gaps had been blown in the wire fences or a minefield had been cleared of explosives, the engineers marked safe paths through the obstacles with strands of white tape.

initial use by June 9. Then, disaster: a monster storm roared along the coast on June 19-20, sinking the U.S. harbor off Omaha Beach. The British Mulberry, christened "Port Winston" and erected off Arromanches, survived. Across its piers, in 100 days, rolled 2.5 million men, 500,000 vehicles and 4 million tons of supplies. Designed to last three months, it did eight months of duty. Today, visitors to Arromanches still marvel at the sunken remains of this colossal creation.

The next challenge: How to supply the gas to run those half-million vehicles—jeeps, tanks, half-tracks, bulldozers and more—that crossed the Mulberries? The answer: Operation Pluto, the pipeline under the ocean, bypassing the threat posed to surface tankers by German submarines. Once the port city of Cherbourg was taken, Pluto became operational, connecting pumping stations (disguised as beach huts) on the Isle of Wight to France; the pipeline finally pumped more than 1 million gallons of fuel to Allied forces. If the battle of Waterloo was won on the playing fields of Eton, the battle of D-day was won in part on the drawing boards of engineers—and in the bathtubs of ocean liners. ∎

> "Amphibious tanks! This must be the Allies' secret weapon!"
> —Lieutenant Jahnke, German officer, Utah Beach

1300-1400 Hours

The Machines

SITUATION REPORT **Sword Beach** British forces capture Sole strongpoint and launch first attack against Hillman strongpoint • **Gold Beach** German forces have begun a limited retreat to prepared defensive positions • **Juno Beach** Canadian troops are expanding the beachhead • **The Enemy** German general Dietrich Kraiss files an erroneous report to headquarters, stating that the invasion has been stopped at every point on Omaha Beach except Colleville

---

LEUTENANT JAHNKE OF THE 709TH DIVISION, 919TH Regiment couldn't believe his eyes—the eyes that watched a huge Allied tank swim out of the English Channel and clank right onto the shore, its treads grinding into the sand. "Here was a truly lunatic sight," the German officer recalled after the war. "I wondered if I were hallucinating as a result of the bombardment. Amphibious tanks! This must be the Allies' secret weapon!"

Jahnke wasn't crazy, but at his post on Utah Beach he was among the first Germans to encounter one of the more inventive war machines of D-day, an amphibious tank. A 33-ton U.S. Sherman with a watertight body, the "swimming tank" carried a canvas flotation collar that could be raised on steel arms to cover the tank's upper area, while displacing enough water to make it float. A duplex-drive (DD) engine powered the tank both in the water and on land. U.S. soldiers christened the colossal amphibians "Donald Ducks."

The swimming tank was only one of the exotic menagerie of war machines developed in World War II, the first fully mechanized war. Today, almost 60 years after the combat ended, the iconic weapons of the war are the clanking tank, the roaring long-distance bomber and the mighty aircraft carrier, but thousands of other weapons were built and deployed in the war, and many of them saw action on D-day.

By 1300 hours on June 6, the beaches of Normandy were swarming with an amazing assortment of specialized Allied tanks. Some had giant rotating cylinders in front, which flailed the beaches with iron chains, detonating mines. Others

LONG-DISTANCE WAR: British troops hauled huge ack-ack guns to Normandy, only to find there were no German planes to fire on. In this picture from August 1944, they are using the big guns to harass German infantry troops

Hobart's Funnies

General Percy Hobart's specialized tanks proved highly valuable on D-day. This page shows five of the adaptations: most of them were built onto British Churchill tanks, though the DD tanks were U.S. Shermans. Versions of "Hobart's Funnies" not shown here include Armored Ramp Carriers (ARCs), a tank with its top chopped off, whose flat superstructure supported two unfolding runways that formed a seawall-bridging roadway. "Bobbin" tanks had a giant spool on the front, on which was rolled a 110-yd.-long carpet of coir, a coarse material made from the husks of coconuts. Deployed under the tank's treads, the coir surface helped the tank gain traction on soft, slippery clay. Armored Towing Vehicles (ARVs) had winches and pulleys to haul crippled vehicles out of combat.

A cable holds a 30-ft. bridge that can support a 40-ton load

A tank with a cylinder of fascines in place

A tank rolls over an antitank ditch filled by fascines

A duplex-drive tank with its canvas skirts up

A duplex-drive tank deploys in a test

A flailing tank with chains hoisted

Some armored ramp carriers unfolded; this one does not

Makeshift teeth helped tanks chew hedgerows

carried large bundles of sticks—fascines—in front, which they dropped into antitank ditches, then proceeded to roll across. Sill others carried their own bridging systems, or winched and towed disabled vehicles off the beach, or lobbed bulky 40-lb. exploding projectiles—"flying dustbins"—at German gun emplacements.

Many of these tanks were conceived and built by a pioneering British general, Percy C.S. Hobart. The British soldiers called his tanks "Hobart's Funnies," and indeed there was something humorous about the big, clumsy tanks tricked out with specialized gadgets: their brute, hulking bodies and dainty appendages were the military equivalent of a rhinoceros in a tutu. Prior to the invasion, American officers were given a chance to watch the "Funnies" in practice runs. They took one look at these highly specialized adaptations and dismissed them as effete, finicky versions of a weapon they considered effective purely as a mobile fortress. The Americans were impressed with the DD amphibious tanks, however, and the swimming Shermans were deployed on every beach on D-day.

A flame-throwing tank chars trees

But most of Hobart's tanks weren't used by the Americans, which is unfortunate: the flailing tanks, in particular, proved highly valuable to the British and Canadians at Sword, Gold and Juno beaches and might have made a big difference at Omaha, where U.S. combat engineers gave their lives to defuse mines—while mines were being harmlessly flailed into oblivion by tanks on nearby beaches. After the war, Dwight Eisenhower said as much, writing, "The comparatively light casualties which we sustained on all the beaches except Omaha were in large measure due to the success of the novel mechanical contrivances which were employed … It is doubtful if the assault forces could have firmly established themselves without the assistance of these weapons." General Eisenhower, it seems, was almost as good a bridge builder as General Hobart. ∎

QUACK! These amphibious 2.5-ton U.S. trucks are not tanks but carriers that hauled troops, artillery and cargo. The DUKWs ("ducks") are one of the few machines of World War II still on active duty; the now-quaint vehicles squire sightseers on water-land journeys at the Boston Common and in other tourist spots

The "Funny" Man

Major General Percy C.S. Hobart was a prickly, brilliant eccentric, the sort of oddball genius who was regarded as highly suspicious by most straight-arrow military men but was particularly prized by the prickly, brilliant eccentric who happened to be the Prime Minister of Britain, Winston Churchill. Hobart was an early and forceful (if undiplomatic) advocate for strategic mobility in armored warfare; beginning in 1934, he created Britain's 1st Tank Brigade, the world's first full-time armored division. Hobart's ideas were later adapted by the Germans in their innovative blitzkrieg strategies, but the quirky theorist was drummed out of the British army by skeptical—perhaps envious—superiors early in 1940.

In August of that year, with the Battle of Britain raging, Churchill read about Hobart in a newspaper story; it noted that Britain's foremost visionary of armored warfare was not on active duty but was serving as a humble corporal in Britain's volunteer Home Guard. The P.M. summoned Hobart to a meeting, took his measure and sent a memo to army brass, noting, "I am not at all impressed by the prejudices against him in certain quarters. Such prejudices attach frequently to persons of strong personality and original view." Wise words indeed from the Cassandra whose warnings of Adolf Hitler's intentions had been widely dismissed in the 1930s.

In March 1943, at age 56, Hobart was asked to take command of what would become known as Britain's 79th (Experimental) Armored Division, and he was encouraged to give free rein to his ideas. Field Marshal Bernard Montgomery, Hobart's brother-in-law, supported "Hobo" and his fantastic bestiary of battlefield beasts. Hobart commanded the 79th Division, which ultimately grew to number some 1,900 armored vehicles, through the battles of Normandy and the Bulge, beyond the Rhine and to victory over Germany in 1945. Vindicated, celebrated and beloved, Hobart was knighted after the war and was mourned as one of Britain's great war heroes at his death in 1957.

1400-1500 Hours

The Chaplains

SITUATION REPORT Omaha Beach With the momentum now firmly in U.S. hands, German gun positions are gradually being subdued and new waves of landing boats are unloading more men on the beach • **Juno Beach** Consolidating their hold over the town of Courseulles after a bitter struggle, Canadian units move south toward Reviers • **Gold Beach** Royal Marine Commandos moving inland south of Arromanches are held up by German fire

ROBERT CAPA—MAGNUM PHOTOS

F IVE WEEKS BEFORE D-DAY, SOME 60 CHAPLAINS FROM various Allied services—including Mike Crooks, a chaplain attached to a Canadian unit scheduled to land at Juno Beach—attended a conference in London. The chaplains were given briefings about what to expect on the beaches and were told to draw morphine from the medical officer of their units. Naval chaplains were issued church pennants, which were to be flown as their ship was standing offshore, to signal their presence to the troops on land. It was an orderly, if solemn, occasion—and thus a long way from the chaos and horror many of these men would face on June 6. The story of the chaplains on D-day is best told by men who excel in story-telling, the chaplains themselves.

In an eloquent sermon he offered at Portsmouth Cathedral in England on June 6, 1997, Crooks looked back to the service he offering after joining his troopship on D-day minus three in England: "On boarding the ship I found that the troops were feeling the strain of waiting. All ships had been loaded and 'sealed' a week previously with nobody allowed to leave— it was stressful. The following morning [Sunday] I had a Holy Communion Service at the intersection of two passages ... difficult! ... like catacombs. This was a momentous occasion, for those communicants were all aware that in a few days time they might be dead—and some of them were. The holy mysteries of Christian Communion probably meant more to them that day in those overcrowded passages than at any other time in their lives. I shall never forget the look in the eyes of some. We were all trimmed down to size at that moment.

"At the end of the service the 'sealed' ship rule was broken for I was given a launch and allowed to go and take prayers and Holy Communion in several other ships. It was a solemn and strenuous day, ending with a Service which I conducted on the ramp in the tank space.

"The following morning [Monday], the long wait ended. The engines came alive, the rumble of the anchor chain and ... we were off. It is impossible to describe the feeling of re-

AMEN: With an organist on duty, a Catholic priest speaks to soldiers; the date is unknown. After his remarks, the priest will don his vestments and say a Mass (see *following page*)

"I prayed like it was only up to God, and I dug like it was only up to me, and together we dug that hole pretty deep."
—Chaplain George R. Barber, who landed on Omaha Beach

medical officers of D-day, who assisted not only the wounded Allies but also the enemy. Crooks' most vivid memory of June 6 is of "the rows of dead German soldiers all carefully laid out on the ground by our orderlies with the contents of their pockets and identity discs in bags attached to their uniforms, subsequently to be sent to their next of kin. They looked so young compared with our more mature soldiers."

WHILE CHAPLAIN CROOKS WAS WATCHING U.S. SAILORS dance with joy at Juno Beach, Chaplain Charles Reed was watching U.S. soldiers dodge bullets at Omaha Beach, where he landed with the 116th Infantry, 29th Division. On that strip of sand, as General Norman Cota is supposed to have said, there were only two types of men that day: those who were dead and those who were about to die.

Reed, then 32, may have felt he was one of the latter group. "I took shelter for a few minutes between a tank and a trailer loaded with ammunition," he told PEOPLE magazine in 1994. "But then the tank started up with no warning and the trailer ran over my right leg, tearing all the ligaments. The only thing that saved the leg from being totally mashed was that I was in the water and sand. I called for help and the medical first sergeant, Arthur Moore, came over to help. He had his arms around me and was pulling me out of danger, when a shell fragment tore his head completely off. I had to leave him in the water because there wasn't anything I could do for him.

"Then I saw this other man 20 to 25 yards out in the channel. The water was over his head, he was floundering. He recognized me and yelled, 'Chaplain, you pray for me.' He needed more than prayer. I was able to swim out and bring him in. He was killed the next day. [By now] my leg was totally black from the knee down. But there were a lot of men dying. The

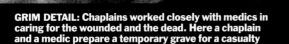

GRIM DETAIL: Chaplains worked closely with medics in caring for the wounded and the dead. Here a chaplain and a medic prepare a temporary grave for a casualty

lief. It was strangely exhilarating. [On D-day morning] we were at our appointed landing place and were ordered to anchor off-shore until the beach-head was secure. My church pennant was now hoisted. A signal came from ashore, SEND IN YOUR CHAPLAIN. Three U.S. sailors delivered me ashore in one of our assault craft. On grounding they dropped the ramp and I was about to step into the water when I was suddenly swept off my feet by two large sailors and planted dry-shod on the sand. Then they began to dance about with boyish delight at being on Juno Beach on D Day. I remember thinking at the time—'I wish to God they would do it somewhere else.'

"I went on my way up the beach … there was a Sherman flailing tank going to and fro exploding mines and I was astounded at the number of the mines, mostly small but occasionally a big one, when the tank would immediately stop (with its chains hanging limply down) whilst the driver had time to recover from the blinding blast and concussion right in front of his face."

Crooks assisted medics in dealing with the injured, prayed with the wounded men and then helped the medics place the dead in temporary graves. Looking back from a vantage point of more than 50 years, he reserved his highest praise for the

ENCOURAGING WORD: U.S. Army Chaplain K. Ale shares a moment with a convalescent soldier at a field hospital in Normandy during the "hedgerow" war after D-day

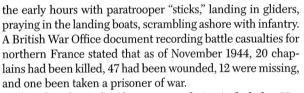

MASS: A soldier prepares to receive Communion at a Catholic Mass on a Normandy beach, where danger dissolved Stateside barriers of denomination and race

first wounded man I ministered to was my organist, Wilson McDiarmid, the only child of a Presbyterian minister. He was lying on the beach—conscious, but breathing his last. I knelt over him, and he recognized me. I said, 'Mac, God is with you.' A smile came over his face, and he was gone."

George R. Barber believes he is the last surviving chaplain who landed at Omaha. His most vivid memory is of seeing a landing craft full of U.S. soldiers explode after colliding with and detonating a mine. Of digging a foxhole, Barber says, "I prayed like it was only up to God, and I dug like it was only up to me, and together we dug that hole pretty deep."

Like their close counterparts the medics, chaplains like Crooks, Reed and Barber went into combat along with the men they counseled, dropping into Normandy in the early hours with paratrooper "sticks," landing in gliders, praying in the landing boats, scrambling ashore with infantry. A British War Office document recording battle casualties for northern France stated that as of November 1944, 20 chaplains had been killed, 47 had been wounded, 12 were missing, and one been taken a prisoner of war.

The adage has it that there are no atheists in foxholes. Nor was there much hand-wringing over sect and denomination among the soldiers and chaplains of Overlord. As Reed recalled, "If I came to a Catholic man, I gave the signs, but I didn't have the power of last rites. I just said a brief prayer. If I recognized they were Jewish, I'd refer to the 23rd, 27th and 21st Psalms of the Old Testament. I'd been with them all through their training in England, so they all knew me personally." Reed turned to the Psalms to comfort himself as well, constantly repeating Psalm 118: "I shall not die, but live and declare the works of the Lord."

In his popular 1994 history of D-day, Stephen Ambrose tells the story of Father Joe Lacy, who went ashore on Omaha. His unit of U.S. Rangers—one of whom called the priest a "small old, fat Irishman"—had urged him to remain at sea during the landing, but Lacy insisted on coming with them. In transit across the Channel on the night of June 5, Lacy told them, "When you land on the beach and you get in there, I don't want to see anybody kneeling down and praying. If I do I'm gonna come up and boot you in the tail. You leave the praying to me and you do the fighting." Such were the chaplains of D-day, living and declaring the works of the Lord. ∎

Artifact

Soldier's Bible

This pocket edition of the New Testament was in the pocket of Private Irwin W. (Turk) Seelye of the 505th Parachute Infantry Regiment when he jumped into Normandy. At the front of the volume is a letter signed by President Roosevelt, "commending the reading of the Bible to all who serve in the armed forces."

The Airmen

SITUATION REPORT Pointe du Hoc U.S. Rangers have set up a perimeter around the captured German fortifications, have assumed defensive positions and are awaiting reinforcement • **Gold Beach** All units have moved inland and are proceeding toward their objectives • **Sword Beach** British forces reach Biéville, but the 3d Division's advance toward Caen stalls because of stubborn German resistance • **The Enemy** Adolf Hitler at last agrees to release the SS panzer divisions he has been holding in reserve

---

A
T 1500 HOURS ON D-DAY, WITH THE SKIES OVERHEAD clearing, 600 aircraft of the U.S. Army Air Force roared over the French coast, bound for the historic city of Caen. Their mission: prepare the way for British ground troops coming off Sword and Gold beaches and heading for the city, eight miles inland from the beaches. As it happened, no Allied troops would reach Caen on June 6; the goal of reaching the city—much less taking control of it— was unrealistic. But the American airmen did their part, as their bombs set the centuries-old buildings of Normandy's largest city afire. It was only the beginning of Caen's woes: the city would be reduced to rubble by the time the Allies won control of it in July.

The afternoon strike on Caen was one of hundreds of supporting runs flown by Allied bombers on D-day. Indeed, Operation Overlord was made possible in large part by the complete superiority of the Allied forces in the skies. Air power was central to the plan: Allied flyers were charged with disrupting German transportation and communications behind the lines before D-day, and with the massive bombing of fixed German positions along the coast in the weeks and months preceding D-day—and in the hours just before the troops landed on the beaches.

Only four years before, the skies over Normandy had been the playground of Luftwaffe fighters and bombers under the command of one of Adolf Hitler's favorite subordinates, Hermann Göring. Day after day, night after night, German planes had swarmed across the Channel to drop their incendiary bombs on London and other cities, opposed only by the outnumbered fighter pilots of the Royal Air Force, the few men— in Churchill's famous phrase—to whom so many owed so much.

But that was in 1940. In the years since the Battle of Britain, America had joined the struggle against the Axis powers and Hitler had declared war on Russia. The week before D-day, LIFE ran a photo of U.S. workers at a Boeing factory in Seattle, inscribing their names on the 5,000th B-17 Flying Fortress built at the plant; in the same week, Lockheed completed

HULTON ARCHIVE—GETTY IMAGES

MISSION ACCOMPLISHED: A Marauder crew is all smiles: their morning bombardment of Utah Beach was a success

work on its 13,000th U.S. war plane. As more and more of these planes arrived in England, and as more and more German flyers were diverted to the Eastern front, the Allies won

"We wouldn't have had to shoot down enemy planes even if they had been there. We would simply have run over them."
—LIFE photographer Frank Scherschel

control of Western Europe's skies. By the spring of 1944, British and American bombers were routinely flying huge raids over Hitler's Germany.

Overlord's planners thus enjoyed a luxury rare in wartime: free of defensive concerns, they debated how best to exploit their complete control of the air. The British—tactical strate-gist Air Vice Marshal Trafford Leigh-Mallory and Air Chief Marshal Arthur Harris of the bomber command—argued for continuing to bomb the oil refineries in Germany that kept the Reich's war machines running. General Dwight Eisenhower disagreed; he believed Allied bombers should attack France's transportation system, crippling the Germans' ability to respond to the landings, thus directly aiding the troops going ashore. When the British wouldn't budge, Ike threatened to resign; he won the support of Churchill, and his Transportation Plan was adopted.

With the debate settled, the British air chiefs embraced Ike's plan: by D-day, Allied planes had dropped some 76,000 tons of bombs on France's railroads. In addition to targeting Normandy, the Allies directed major bombardments on the Pas de Calais area, continuing the massive feint to convince the Germans the invasion would come there. On such runs, the Allied bombers were almost unopposed in the air. But the Germans commanded serious antiaircraft artillery, and the bombing runs were truly frightening for Allied airmen: after long hours of flying in frigid aircraft to reach their targets, they entered a hellish environment of sound, fury and ack-ack fire. LIFE estimated just before D-day that some 3,000 Allied bombers and 1,500 fighters had been lost in the big bombing runs, and some 25,000 American and British airmen were either dead or in prisoner-of-war camps in Germany.

Overlord called for an unprecedented coordination of forces in the air with those on the land and sea. The Allied bomber crews shared a key role with the gun crews aboard the big battleships in the Channel: they would hammer the German fortifications along the coast, silencing the huge guns di-

rected out to sea and onto the beaches, clearing the path for the invaders. Prior to D-day, many Allied infantrymen were assured that the dual bombardments from the sea and air would take out most of the German guns, and that the bombs and shells would create big craters on the beach, ready-made cover from any remaining fire. It all looked good—on paper.

OPERATION OVERLORD CALLED FOR THE BIG, HIGH-FLYING B-17s (Flying Fortresses) and B-24s (Liberators) to attack Omaha and other beaches, and for the low-flying B-26s (Marauders) to target Utah. LIFE photographer Frank Scherschel was aboard one of the Marauders. His account: "[It] was the easiest operational trip I ever made. We thought it was going to be murder but it wasn't. To show you how easy it was, I ate my bar of chocolate. In every other operational trip I sweated so much the chocolate they gave us melted in my breast pocket. After this trip over the beaches I found the chocolate all in one piece.

"At our briefing the CO said, 'This is it,' and everybody yelled like mad Indians. Our target was a battery of six heavy shore guns that would raise hell with the boats coming into the beaches unless they were silenced. We had to lay our bombs down at precisely 6:25, for the troops on our beach were to touch down at exactly that moment.

"It was raining, misty and cold as we got into our ships. We arrived over our target almost five minutes early because of a heavy tail wind, but held our bombs until the appointed time. We had been instructed to go down below cloud level, even if it was 1,000 ft., in order to hit our target right on the nose. Actually we were able to bomb from about 6,000 ft.

"Some flak came up but there were no enemy planes. There were Forts, Liberators, fighters and fighter bombers everywhere—all of them ours. We wouldn't have had to shoot down

BRIEFING: In the first hours of June 6, Marauder crews get flying orders for their support run over Utah Beach

FRANK SCHERSCHEL—TIME LIFE PICTURES

BRITISH WAR MINISTRY

STRAFING RUN: Bristol Beaufighter aircraft attack a convoy of German freighters off the Frisian Islands with rockets, cannons and machine guns

Enter the Rockets

Only two weeks after D-day, TIME reported on a new weapon in Germany's arsenal. "Britain finally felt the lash of Adolf Hitler's long-threatened secret weapon last week," the magazine said, "and found it much like its sponsor: nasty, unpredictable, incapable of achieving final victory. The weapon . . . a self-propelled "robot bomb" . . . has stubby wings (16 ft. across) and tiny tail surface; its only pilot is a gyrocompass control box . . . the bomb is driven by a cleverly designed jet propulsion engine . . . Speed is about 300 m.p.h.; maximum range possibly 150 miles."

Hitler used the V-1 rocket (or "buzz-bomb") as an instrument of terror, bombing London from across the Channel with it; he later did the same with the much larger V-2 rocket. World War II was the first war in which rockets were deployed. The Soviets pioneered their use with the Katyusha artillery rocket-launcher, nicknamed "Stalin's organ." The British began equipping their Bristol Beaufighter airplanes with small underwing rockets in 1944, and U.S. planes soon carried them.

The months after D-day saw the introduction of two paradigm-shattering weapons that would completely alter the future of combat. In July 1944 the Luftwaffe sent the first jet fighter, the Messerschmitt Me-262, into battle. In August 1945 the U.S. devastated Hiroshima and Nagasaki with atom bombs to end the war in Japan.

BRITISH WAR MINISTRY

FOUR-PACK: Ground crews hang rockets on the guide rails of a Beaufighter. The airplane-carried weapon was adapted from antiaircraft rockets

Artifact

Bomb Tag

Asa Clark, a pilot with the U.S. Ninth Air Force, made a run over Utah Beach on D-day to support the landings. Clark's habit was to keep track of his missions by jotting down notes on the small paper ID tag that came with each bomb and was removed when it was armed. The sortie over Utah Beach on June 6 was Clark's 45th mission (he would fly 70); on the tag he wrote, "The big show is on."

less effective in reality. The weather was harsh at dawn's early light; a patchy cloud cover separated bomber convoys and limited the bombardiers' visibility. In addition, many of the bombardiers who were able to see landing craft bobbing in the waves below became gun-shy, afraid of taking Allied lives with friendly fire. As a result—especially at Omaha—much of the ordnance dropped by the planes landed a mile or two inland from the beach, where better, more accurate air support might have helped save lives.

Some infantry troops who had been oversold on the power of preinvasion air support held the airmen responsible for the carnage on shore, but that is an understandably shortsighted view. The naval fleet's big guns definitely played a stronger role than the air forces' big bombs in helping Allied soldiers ashore in the first, terrible hours of D-day. But the Allied airmen made Overlord possible in the first place with their hard-won control of the skies. That advantage played out in ways large and small: when General Erwin Rommel learned of the landings while in Germany, he was unable to fly back to Normandy for fear his plane might be shot down by Allied fighters. The Reich's best man was missing in action on D-day, hamstringing the German response—thanks to air power. ∎

enemy planes even if they had been there. We would simply have run over them."

The Marauders' bombs helped the U.S. troops take Utah Beach with minimum loss of life. These bombers flew low, offering their crews a good view of the target. But the B-17s and B-24s flew at 20,000 ft., high above the fray, and their preinvasion bombing runs were not as effective as the Marauder sorties; the plan that had looked so good on paper proved far

THE B-17 "FLYING FORTRESS" BOMBER

Astronavagation dome

Hand-held gun

Bombardier

Plastic nose

Chin gun turret

Ammunition

HF radio antenna

Direction-finding antenna

Engine

Pilot and Co-pilot

Oxygen

Upper gun turret

Bombs

Navigator

Radio operator

Bomb door

The Saturation Man

In the picture above, only the uniform of British Air Chief Marshal Arthur Harris reveals his military rank; otherwise, intently studying a file, he might be taken for an insurance actuary. The statistics of death were, in fact, his business: "Bomber" Harris was the architect of Britain's "area bombing" campaign, the plan that sent Allied planes on long bombing runs deep into the heart of industrial Germany. At first those raids targeted factories; later they devastated churches, schools and homes. As a result, Harris remains one of the most controversial Allied commanders of the conflict; he has been called a war criminal, and not only by Germans.

Reared in Rhodesia and educated in Britain, Harris served in the Royal Flying Corps in World War I and remained in the Royal Air Force between wars. He was named to lead the R.A.F. bombing efforts in 1942, amid dissatisfaction with Britain's air campaign. He soon developed his strategy of "saturation bombing," staging huge raids over Germany with as many as 1,000 bombers. Initially, the bombs fell on Germany's factories, oil refineries and railroads, but Harris increasingly argued that his planes could bomb the German people into submission, and his incendiary bombs now fell on civilian neighborhoods. The tactics were not unlike the "total war" practiced by Hitler in the Battle of Britain, and they generated enormous controversy among the Allies.

As Overlord took shape, Harris squared off against Dwight Eisenhower, angry that he might have to direct his bombers against French railroads rather than German cities. But once Harris was ordered to support the Transportation Plan, he threw himself into it with gusto. He stayed in his post until the war's end, though his tactics—like the deadly 1945 fire-bombings of Dresden and Hamburg—drew mounting scorn in Britain. Strongly criticized after the war, Harris defended himself in his 1947 autobiography, *Bomber Offensive*. He died in 1984.

This long-range heavy bomber was the U.S. workhorse of World War II. Its unpressurized cabin had no climate control, leaving its oxygen-masked crew exposed to extremes of heat and cold. Of the 12,731 B-17s made by Boeing, more than a third were shot down by enemy fire, and more than 40,000 airmen were injured, captured or killed. But the B-17 was also sturdy. Stories of Flying Fortresses limping home with one or more engines dead, large pieces of wing shot off, or with gaping holes in the fuselage made the big bomber a legend.

Dorsal fin

Rudder

Tail gunner

Ammunition

Waist gunner

Ammunition

Oxygen

Door

Sperry ball-gun turret

Ammunition

Door

Toilet

Tail wheel

Door

297976

K

O

1600-1700 Hours

The Quartermasters

SITUATION REPORT **Omaha Beach** German resistance in Coleville draw is finally subdued
• **Juno/Sword Beaches** The 21st Panzer Division finally is ordered to launch a counter-attack. It meets British troops moving inland, beginning a pitched battle during which the 21st will lose several tanks • **Gold Beach** A German task force advances on Bayeux to attack British forces; its commander is killed in the battle and the German unit withdraws

SHORTLY AFTER 4 P.M. ON JUNE 6, ONE OF THE VERY FEW men who was not assigned to an airborne unit but who had nonetheless landed behind Utah Beach in an American glider achieved his objective for D-day. Sergeant Elbert Legg of the 603rd Quartermaster Company had been searching for a field to match the specifications in his order since just before noon, when his glider had come to a very rough landing near the crossroads of Les Forges. He had no idea where the field would turn out to be located, for no map could pinpoint its location. But he did know its approximate size and was sure that it wouldn't be far from where the first gliders touched down. Most of all, Legg knew that this field would have to be close enough to the front lines to be a short journey for the American soldiers who would make use of it, yet far enough away for the solemn work that would be done there to proceed undisturbed. Legg was searching for a place to establish the first Allied cemetery in France.

The location he chose was next to an apple orchard just outside the village of Blosville, a few miles south of Ste.-Mère-Eglise—one of the first towns to be liberated by Allied invaders and the scene of some of the first combat deaths. The meadow Legg chose already contained four dead paratroop-ers, who had fallen there earlier in the day. Working quickly, he broke apart a crate (which had contained K rations) into wooden stakes and began measuring plots by pacing the length and breadth of the field. In the time that it took Legg to mark the space for 20 graves, the word was out: jeeps and trucks bearing more Allied dead drove into the field and left 14 more bodies. Within the hour, a lieutenant who had been assigned the task of coordinating the burial of the 82nd Airborne's dead returned with the news that he had recruited 35 French civilians from Ste.-Mère-Eglise to begin digging graves in the morning. Their cooperation had been secured, Legg would later recall, when "he displayed a musette bag full of 'invasion francs' intended for

JUNE 9: The coxswain of a supply ferry—most likely the sort of "rhino" ferry shown on the next pages—gets a bird's-eye view of a landing beach from atop his wheelhouse

"They help unload ships right at the dock ...

Hardly a day goes by without casualties ...

But they take this bombing and shelling bravely."

—Ernie Pyle

JUNE 7: Quartermaster Corps troops unload supplies. The efforts of black soldiers in World War II helped put an end to the longtime segregation of the U.S. military

supply side of Operation Overlord in August 1943. As TIME reported of a little noticed aspect of the Channel crossing, "In the invasion fleet were some 300 private boats of from 275- to 3,500-ton capacity, which had to be loaded long before D-day, tagged for specific landing areas and kept ready to sail. There had to be a loading priority plan so that supplies could be unloaded as needed in those first critical and tumultuous hours." So essential was Lutes' contribution to Overlord that, after he had returned to Washington, his work seemingly complete, in the weeks before D-day, General Eisenhower requested that he come back to England and inspect the preparations one last time. Only then did Eisenhower proceed with the invasion planning.

For Overlord, the Quartermaster Corps not only brought supplies to the front lines but also invented new equipment to do so, such as integrated, roller-bearing conveyors that allowed Allied troops on the invasion beaches to slide bulky car-

that purpose." Two days later, these Frenchman would be replaced by German prisoners, for whom payment was unnecessary. Within weeks, the bodies of more than 6,000 Allied fighting men would come to rest in the field.

Burying the dead was but one of the mundane but essential chores carried out with silent heroism by the Allied quartermasters, the support personnel who were also responsible for ensuring that everything a man in uniform needs to continue fighting is there when he reaches for it. The Quartermaster Corps supplied invasion troops with food, clothing and medical supplies, kept vehicles loaded with fuel and worked with ordnance specialists to ensure that every Allied weapon—from Colt .45 pistols to howitzers—never fell silent for lack of ammunition.

The statistics are mind-boggling. The "Outline of Operation Overlord" called for quartermasters to land, in the first 24 hours of D-day, 175,000 men, 1,500 tanks and 10,000 trucks on the beaches. Behind this effort was Pentagon logistics expert Major General LeRoy Lutes, who began working on the

CHOW TIME: U.S. Army nurses at a field hospital take time out for an al fresco lunch of C rations. The diner in back appears to have some reservations about the fare

TRAILHEAD: Troops move materiél in a massive supply depot in England, location undisclosed, before D-day

tons directly off boats and onto dry land faster (and dryer) than troops could have carried them. And existing technologies were put to dramatic new uses, as when the Quartermaster Railhead Companies built railroad tracks from existing Normandy train lines down onto the invasion beaches, where specialized landing craft could offload entire freight cars full of supplies directly onto the beach.

Army lore claimed an assignment to the QM Corps was a "safe billet," but Colonel Andrew McNamara, Chief Quartermaster for the First Army, recalled that his troops "performed every type of truck support for the fighting troops of the 82nd and 101st Airborne divisions. Supplies were taken up into front lines and unloaded directly to user units, with the bulk of the missions being completed under shellfire and strafing."

But there is more to the story of the Quartermaster Corps: it was one of the handful of war assignments in which African-American soldiers could expect to see action. In the strictly segregated U.S. Army of the 1940s, all officers and almost all

NCOs were white. But the Quartermaster Corps was one of the handful of units to which black enlistees were funneled. African Americans made up the bulk of many of the quartermaster units that served at the front lines on June 6, performing such essential duties as burying corpses and unloading supplies while German artillery thundered overhead.

A few months earlier, Ernie Pyle had written glowingly (albeit in the insensitive argot of the day) about black quartermaster troops in the Anzio invasion: "Around seventy percent of the Quartermaster troops on the beachhead are colored boys. They help unload ships right at the dock ... Hardly a day goes by without casualties among them. But they take this bombing and shelling bravely. They make an awful lot of funny remarks about it, but they take it." The efforts of such men were rewarded in 1948, when a tough World War I veteran—President Harry S. Truman—ended the segregation of the U.S. military with a single, decisive Executive Order.

On D-day, quartermasters troops—both black and white—took enemy fire bravely. By the time D-day plus one (June 7) drew to a close, Sergeant Legg was overseeing the burial of members of the Quartermaster Corps at his newly established cemetery in Blosville. Before the war in Europe ended, all the bodies interred there would be moved to a larger, permanent Allied cemetery in Normandy or, in some cases, returned to the U.S. or Britain for burial. But today a small monument at the Les Forges crossroads marks the field beside the apple orchard where the first Americans to fall in the battle for France came to rest. ∎

Artifact

K Ration

Abused, denounced, deplored—but eaten—the K ration is one of the undying icons of World War II. Developed for paratroopers by Dr. Ancel Keys (hence the K) at the University of Minnesota, this "emergency combat field ration" might include canned ham spread, bouillon cubes, gum, sausage and a chocolate bar.

JUNE 6: Towed by a tug, a "rhino" ferry—a floating barge—bears large equipment across the Channel. Ferries did much of the heavy lifting of the invasion

NORMANDY, 1944

"The long sobs of the violins of autumn / Wound my heart with a monotonous languor." —Couplet by Paul Verlaine that alerted the Resistance to the coming invasion

The French

SITUATION REPORT **Omaha Beach** Americans tanks begin moving through the St. Laurent Draw • **Sword Beach** British forces begin a second attack on Hillman strongpoint; a second unit reaches the outskirts of Lébisey Forest • **Juno Beach** Canadian forces reach Bény-sur-Mer, three miles inland • **The Enemy** General Erwin Rommel is in his staff car, en route back to Normandy from Germany

ROBERT HUNT LIBRARY

TO HEAR THE TWO GENERALS' DUELING DECLARATIONS to the French public on June 6 is to sense the tension and rivalry that marked the uneasy alliance between Dwight Eisenhower and Charles de Gaulle. Broadcasting from England just before 1800 hours, Eisenhower announced, "I am proud to have again under my command the gallant forces of France. Fighting beside their allies, they will play a worthy part in the liberation of their homeland." Eisenhower also warned that "a premature uprising of all Frenchmen may prevent you from being of maximum help to your country in the critical hour. Be patient. Prepare."

In a radio speech beamed into France from England less than an hour later, General De Gaulle, leader of the French Forces of the Interior, substituted messianic fervor for Ike's caution. Calling the invasion both "the Battle of France" and "the Battle of the French," he noted in passing, "We are told that an immense assault force has begun to leave the shores of Old England to aid us," and he exclaimed that "for the sons of France, it goes without saying, the obligation is simple and sacred, to fight with all the means at their disposal."

De Gaulle thus not only dispensed with Eisenhower's "command" of French troops but also seemed to relegate the Americans, British and Canadians who made up the vast majority of the invasion force to the status of supporting players. Three days before the invasion, Eisenhower's staff had asked De Gaulle to make a speech following Ike's, counseling his countrymen to follow the Supreme Commander's orders. De Gaulle, TIME reported, "exclaimed 'I cannot follow Eisenhower!' Then he turned on his polished heel and strode off. Behind him he left turmoil. No one knew just what he meant: whether he would not 'follow Eisenhower' on the air, or in principle, or both." That night, as De Gaulle wrote his speech without consulting Ike, Eisenhower would confide to his diary that the French general topped his list of worries about Operation Overlord.

But if De Gaulle was infuriating, the Resistance forces he led were invaluable, making an enormous difference to the outcome of D-day—or, as the French called it, *"J-jour."* By the

ENTENTE CORDIALE: French Resistance fighters confer with Allied troops during the Battle of Normandy. Ike said the aid of the Resistance was worth five divisions on D-day

HEROES: At left is Marc Marinaut, who saved the life of Private Eason, the U.S. paratrooper at right, who landed around 0230 in Normandy. Between them is Mlle. Nicole Celebonovitch, who linked up with paratroopers and led them to a group of hidden Germans on D-day

regularly made the trip from Courseulles to Isigny, passing nondescript stretches of sand that are now best remembered by the names Juno, Gold and Omaha. German guards would occasionally challenge him but would allow him to pass when he produced a license issued by the French Federation of Bicycle Racers. Mercader was mentally noting the position and size of every large gun emplacement on his route. His reports, along with those made by dozens of agents reporting to him, helped Operation Overlord planners decide which beaches would make the best sites for landing troops.

I N THE FIRST WEEK OF JUNE, AGENTS OF THE CENTURIE AT last heard an announcement they had been anticipating for months. Straining over wireless sets they had concealed from the Germans, Resistance fighters heard a BBC announcer recite the first half of a couplet from poet Paul Verlaine, "the long sobs of the violins of autumn ..." several evenings in a row. This was a cue to indicate that a major announcement was coming soon. At last, on the evening of June 5, the BBC announcer recited the first line from Verlaine again but this time joined it to the next line: "... wound my heart with a monotonous languor." This meant that the invasion was imminent and that Centurie members should now unleash the wave of violence they had so long suppressed in favor of gathering information.

On the evening of June 5 and during the early-morning hours of June 6, Resistance members in and around Normandy staged more than 1,000 separate attacks: sabotaging every bridge on the River Seine between Paris and the English Channel (greatly delaying the Germans in bringing reinforcements to the front, and preventing those Germans close to the Channel from retreating), blowing up 950 sections of railroad track (slowing German deployments) and setting up roadside ambushes in which German troop convoys were sprayed with machine-gun fire. They also engaged in countless smaller but potent acts of sabotage, such as cutting telephone and telegraph lines, hindering German communication.

"THEY WENT THATAWAY": French civilians provide information on German troop locations to green-bereted commandos of Britain's 4th S.S. Brigade in the streets of St.-Aubin-sur-Mer in the morning hours of June 6. The troops have just landed and moved off Sword Beach

spring of 1944, the Resistance had established cells inside every large city and most small villages in occupied France. The Maquis (as the Resistance was known nationally) regularly staged acts of sabotage and assassination against German targets. But in Normandy (where it was called "Centurie") the Resistance had been ordered to avoid overt acts that would arouse German attention or retribution, and instead focus almost exclusively on gathering intelligence.

An unassuming Norman housepainter, Rene Duchez, came home one evening in late 1942 and announced to his wife Odette that "I've just played a good trick on the Germans." Duchez had been hired to paint offices at the French coastal headquarters of the Todt Organization, the German construction authority responsible for designing and building the Atlantic Wall. When the opportunity arose, Duchez stole a complete set of plans to the fortifications between the port of Cherbourg and the Seine estuary, which were smuggled to England. The plans played a vital role in dissuading Overlord planners from their initial idea of assaulting one of the heavily fortified harbors, like Cherbourg.

Another Norman, Guillaume Mercader, seemed harmless to the Germans. The owner of a chain of bicycle shops, he also competed in cycle races, for which he trained by riding over the bluffs and cliffs of the Normandy coast. Mercader

As the scale of both the invasion and the Resistance uprising became clear, Marshal Philippe Pétain, the aging, puppet head of France's collaborationist Vichy regime, made his own address to the French people on June 6, urging citizens not to rise up against the Germans for fear of reprisals. Pétain's pleas went unheeded, but he was right about the reprisals. Within hours of the first paratrooper landings, the local Gestapo led the 90 Resistance prisoners it was holding at a prison in Caen into a courtyard and executed them.

After France was liberated, Eisenhower would reflect that the activities of the Resistance had been worth the equivalent of five Allied divisions. De Gaulle would probably have argued that it was the Allied troops who were assisting him, not the other way around. When Paris was taken on Aug. 25, he exulted, "Paris! Paris insulted! Paris broken! Paris martyred! Paris freed! Paris freed by itself, freed by its own people with the assistance of the armies of France, with the support and assistance of the entire French nation …" The supporting players from "Old England" whom De Gaulle mentioned in his June 6 broadcast had apparently been demoted.

With the Germans gone, the French turned to the business of purging their own ranks of those now deemed traitors. Men who had collaborated with the Germans were, as often as not, executed—as were German prisoners who fell into the hands

JUNE 17: U.S. troops offer welcome medicine—candy— to a French child wounded in the Battle of Normandy

of French civilians. Women who had fraternized or collaborated with the occupiers suffered the public humiliation of having their heads shaved. Disgraced politicians fared little better. The 89-year-old Marshal Pétain was spared execution but was sentenced to life imprisonment. His partner in collaboration, Occupation Prime Minister Pierre Laval, was less fortunate: he faced a firing squad in October 1945. ∎

DISGRACED: Shaved of their hair and stripped of their dresses, Frenchwomen who slept with German troops or otherwise collaborated are displayed in a public parade

Y 1830 HOURS ON D-DAY, LIEUT. VINCENT SCHLOTTER-beck of the 336th Combat Engineers had been in an LST for more than 14 hours. "We had loaded onto the ships that would take us to the beach at about 4 in the morning," the 86-year-old Ohio native recalls. Schlotterbeck (now a retired Chrysler customer-relations manager) and his unit were assigned to land on Omaha Beach. "But all day," he recalls, "they kept waving us back, which told me there were horrible things happening on that beach. So we kept circling and looking for a place to land."

"Our coxswain was so panicked, he tried to dump us in deep water, then tried to bring us into the beach next to a burning cargo ship loaded with ammunition. We finally had to point our rifles at him and tell him that if he didn't get hold of himself, we'd throw him over the side and take the LST in ourselves."

It wasn't until after 6 in the evening that the landing craft carrying Schlotterbeck, another 20 men, half a dozen jeeps and two Piper Cubs finally found a clear approach to the beach. "But just as we're starting to line up with the clear lane," he recalls, "another big landing craft races for the same slot and cuts in front of us. It was an LCIL," Schlotterbeck says. "Landing Craft Infantry Large. Those boats could hold almost 200 men."

As the LCIL proceeded to shore ahead of Schlotterbeck's vessel, a German 88-mm artillery emplacement on shore fired and scored a direct hit. "It was horrible," Schlotterbeck says. "About a dozen men made it over the side. We never saw them again. I have no idea whether they lived or died." But he does know what happened to the 170 or so men who remained onboard. "A few seconds later, the same gun landed another direct hit on the boat," he says. "Then a third, and a

THE PRICE: After D-day, with Omaha Beach safely in Allied hands, troops regard fallen comrades. Disposition of the dead was orderly in Overlord; these bodies will soon be buried in temporary graves or sent to England for burial

1800-1900 Hours

The Fallen

SITUATION REPORT Omaha Beach American forces moving inland capture St. Laurent • **Sword Beach** British forces moving off the beach reach Bellevue and Bénouvile • **Pointe du Hoc** Germans stage a counterattack against the Rangers, who hold out but sustain heavy losses • **Airborne Operations** A new wave of gliders, carrying troops of Britain's 6th Airborne Division, takes off from England

fourth." In the space of a few seconds, the LCIL was reduced to an inferno of twisted steel, burning fuel and exploding ordnance from which no one could escape. "We sat there watching helplessly," Schlotterbeck recalls, "as more than one hundred men died."

Minutes later, Schlotterbeck's LST beached successfully and he beheld the carnage that was Omaha. "We had to get up the bluff," he said. "But we couldn't get to the base of the rise without walking on dead Americans." Schlotterbeck proceeded as gingerly as he could, at one point stepping forward over the body of a fallen American soldier who was lying face-up. "Just as I was about to put my foot down," Schlotterbeck recalls, "he opened his eyes. I almost did a back-flip trying to avoid stepping on him, but I managed not to touch him. From

"Our sons, pride of our nation, this day have set upon a mighty endeavor ... Some will never return. Embrace these, Father, and receive them."

President Franklin D. Roosevelt, radio address, June 6

the shape he was in, I don't think he survived," Schlotterbeck says, his voice catching even 60 years later. "But I hope I didn't make those last few minutes worse for him."

At Omaha Beach alone, more than 2,000 Americans died on June 6. The total number of Allied fatalities on D-day is not known with any precision—mostly because the chaos of battle prevented Graves Registration personnel from distinguishing between deaths that occurred on the day itself and those that immediately followed. But the most reliable estimates put the figure somewhere between 3,000 and 5,000. The German military would later estimate that almost double that number from their own ranks perished in the first 24 hours of Operation Overlord.

Canadian authorities say that fewer than 500 of their countrymen died on D-day; the number of Britons is placed at between 2,500-3,000. The first of them was most likely Den Brotheridge of Britain's 6th Airborne Division. Shortly after midnight, Brotheridge landed in a glider outside Ouistreham and led his platoon in the successful assault on what is now known as Pegasus Bridge. A natural athlete so gifted that it was widely assumed he would become a professional football (soccer) player after the war, Brotheridge led the charge from the front and was the first to cross the bridge. He was also the first to fall, cut down with a bullet to the neck by one of the bridge's fleeing German defenders. According to the divisional medic, he looked "very surprised, terribly surprised."

IN THE DAYS FOLLOWING JUNE 6, MOST AMERICANS WERE exhilarated that the long-promised invasion had begun at last. But there was little celebration in Bedford, Va. The quiet farm town in the Blue Ridge Mountains (pop. 3,400) wasn't unpatriotic; it was apprehensive. In the 1940s, the U.S. Army often assigned recruits from the same town or region to a single unit. Consequently, most of the infantrymen that Bedford provided to the U.S. war effort were assigned to a single outfit, Company A of the 116th Infantry, 29th Division.

As the sun rose on June 6, the 180 men of Company A (about 1 in 6 was from Bedford) were heading for the Dog Green sector of Omaha Beach. Their commanding officer, Captain Taylor Fellers, the son of a wealthy Bedford family, confided quietly to one of his lieutenants that they were facing "certain slaughter." Fellers made a point of touching each

WORK DETAIL: Two German prisoners dig temporary graves to hold the bodies of both Allied and German soldiers outside the town of St.-Laurent-sur-Mer

HOMEWARD-BOUND: After landing in the first wave at Omaha Beach, LIFE photographer Robert Capa returned to England on a hospital ship, where he took this picture of medics placing the dead in orderly rows on deck

ROBERT CAPA—MAGNUM PHOTOS

of the men in his command on the shoulder as they boarded the landing craft. It was a fitting last gesture: Fellers was among the first to die when the front ramp of his LST dropped onto the sands of Omaha Beach and all 29 passengers on the landing craft were machine-gunned to death in a matter of seconds. More landing craft followed; within an hour, more than half of Company A (a total of 103 men) were dead.

As the Western Union telegraph at Green's Drugstore in Bedford hummed with traffic in the days following June 6, the town's collective apprehension turned to stunned grief. Among the 34 sons of Bedford who had gone ashore on D-day, 19 had died in action. (Three more would follow in the Battle of Normandy.)

"We got the first one on Sunday [June 11]," Lucille Hoback Boggess would later recall of the notification that Bedford Hoback, one of her two brothers who landed on Omaha, had been killed in action. "And then Monday, the following day, we received a second telegram saying that Raymond was missing in action." Raymond Hoback's body was never found, but in the surf that washed his remains out to sea, another soldier from Company A found the Bible that the soldier had carried with him and sent it to Hoback's parents.

Bedford natives Clyde Powers and Roy Stevens were slated to go ashore together on June 6, but their boat was turned back in the chaos of the first few hours at Omaha. When they finally landed on the beach, five days later, each heard that his brother had been wounded. So the pair went looking for John Powers and Ray Stevens but couldn't locate them at any of the makeshift aid stations that dotted the beach. Finally, Clyde and Roy found their brothers' dogtags dangling from crosses

in a temporary cemetery. The two boyhood friends had been laid to rest next to each other.

THE NILAND BROTHERS OF TONAWANDA, N.Y., WERE among the very few sets of three siblings to fight in Normandy. Robert Niland, 29, parachuted with the 82nd Airborne into Ste.-Mère-Eglise, where he died when he refused to abandon a wounded comrade as the Germans advanced on their position. His younger brother Preston, a 25-year-old lieutenant in the 4th Infantry, was cut down by a German sniper on Utah Beach as he searched for two missing G.I.s. The youngest Niland brother, 24-year-old Frederick, jumped with the 101st Airborne, landing near Carentan.

Days later, hearing that Robert had been killed, Frederick drove to every Allied burial ground he could find, looking for his brother's remains. When he was told at one cemetery that "the only Niland here is a Preston Niland," the full magnitude of his family's loss dawned on Frederick. When the War Department realized what had befallen the Niland family, it ordered Frederick (who protested that "I'm staying here with my boys") sent home. Members of the Niland family were honored guests at the opening of the 1998 film Saving Private Ryan, which echoed their story.

The grief of families like the Hobacks, the Powers and the Nilands was far from unique. During Operation Overlord, 33 sets of brothers would be killed, as would a father and son. But for every name and every story that has become part of D-day lore, there are countless more whose stories we cannot know. In Normandy's Allied cemeteries, there are hundreds of headstones that read, HERE RESTS IN HONORED GLORY A COMRADE IN ARMS KNOWN BUT TO GOD, marking the interment of fallen soldiers who were never identified. The Garden of the Missing contains the inscribed names of more than 1,500 Allied soldiers whose remains were never found. About this hallowed ground, television commentator Andy Rooney (who landed at Normandy as a young reporter for Stars and Stripes) would write a half-century later, "If you think the world is selfish and rotten, go to the cemetery at Colleville overlooking Omaha Beach. See what one group of men did for another on June 6, 1944." ∎

THE FIRST MEMORIAL: Shortly after D-day, French civilians join Allied troops for a memorial Mass on Omaha Beach near the town of Colleville-sur-Mer

ROBERT CAPA—MAGNUM PHOTOS

1900-2000 Hours

The Enigma Machine

SITUATION REPORT Omaha Beach The Vierville Draw and the Les Moulins Draw are now open. Allied engineers are clearing a path for vehicles through the Coleville Draw • **Gold Beach** The British 50th Division has advanced from the beachhead to the outskirts of Bayeaux • **Sword Beach** The 21st Panzer Division has reached the sea between Lion and Luc sur Mer, but a lack of reinforcements forces the German tanks to withdraw from this vital salient between Sword and Juno Beaches

AT 7:15 P.M., A GERMAN COMMANDER IN GENERAL Gert von Runstedt's headquarters was handed a message sent via the Germans' top-secret Enigma coding machine. Decoded, it read, "surprise landing in Oslo [a German code word for an area many miles southwest of Normandy] to be reckoned with." In fact, there were no Allied troops landing in this area, near the town of Granville; the message reflected the utter confusion that reigned behind German lines. Yet the Germans nonetheless diverted their forces to defend the town and blow up its harbor, in the mistaken belief that it was surrounded by American paratroopers. A snafu? Yes. But the most fascinating aspect of the misbegotten message is this: it was read by the Allies at the same time it was read by von Runstedt's staff.

Here was one of the great secrets of World War II: throughout the conflict, the Allies had access to secret German communications, thanks to their mastery of the Enigma code machine. In fact, the very existence of the Enigma machine was so secret that it was not made public until 25 years after the war ended. To tell its story properly, we must begin four years before D-day.

On the afternoon of Nov. 14, 1940, Winston Churchill, normally the most decisive of men, was wracked by agonizing indecision. Ironically, his dilemma was created by two pieces of good news. The first, known to almost everyone in England, was that by late 1940, the Battle of Britain had largely been won. German bombers attacked London less frequently and in smaller numbers. The second was England's most closely guarded secret of the war: Germany's radio codes had been broken, and British spies were reading Hitler's orders to his generals on the ground, in the air and on the high seas at will. Within hours, these two encouraging developments would come together to claim more than 500 lives, affect the outcome of the war and haunt Churchill for the rest of his life.

By the autumn of 1940, Hermann Göring's Luftwaffe was in tatters. The waves of fighters that the Royal Air Force sent to meet every incoming wave of German bombers, combined with increasingly precise ground defenses, meant that the

Germans could no longer mount large-scale raids on London and still hope to emerge with most of their force intact. Turning to less heavily defended targets, the Luftwaffe began to bomb the industrial Midlands north of London.

This change of strategy preoccupied a team of mathematicians, linguists, hieroglyphics scholars, crossword-puzzle enthusiasts and assorted other savants who had been assembled in secret at an estate called Bletchley Park shortly after the war began. Within a few months of England's declaration of war on Germany, they had begun to chip away at the German code reserved for the most secret military traffic, Enigma.

One year into the war, the Bletchley Park team could decipher almost any encoded German transmission in a matter of minutes. And now the team was picking up coded references to a large-scale bombing raid against an industrial target in the next 48 hours. The Germans had code-named the raid Moonlight Sonata. The target: Coventry, a quiet city of more than 100,000 people, largely untouched by German air raids up to that time. Located in England's industrial center, it housed aircraft and tank production as well as several engine factories. Its Cathedral of St. Michael was considered one of England's finest examples of Gothic architecture.

Late on the afternoon of Nov. 14, the codebreakers at Bletchley Park intercepted final instructions to the pilots of the Moonlight Sonata raid: they were to strike Coventry at 7:15 p.m. Word was passed up the chain of command to Churchill, but the information seemed calculated to do little more than frustrate. Two hours' notice didn't leave enough time to evacuate even a small part of the city's population. And if civil defense measures were activated, they would be seen from the air. The Germans would immediately suspect a broken code.

Churchill made up his mind: no alert was given. For one night, the Germans had free rein over the city of Coventry. The Luftwaffe dropped more than 500 tons of high explosives, including 30,000 incendiary bombs. By the time the all-clear siren sounded at 6:20 the following morning, 554 people were dead, the Cathedral of St. Michael was flattened, and Coventry was a smoking ruin. But the most important secret

ROBERT HUNT LIBRARY

"In war-time, truth is so precious that it must be protected by a bodyguard of lies." —Winston Churchill

TOP SECRET: General Heinz Guderian, architect of Germany's blitzkrieg attacks, issues orders in his command car. This is one of the few photographs that shows an Enigma machine in use by the Germans

COLOSSUS, 1944

THE BIG IDEA: Alan Turing's Colossus machine, the world's first programmable binary electronic computer, took up several rooms at Bletchley Park. The women operators were members of the British Women's Royal Naval Service (WRNS); they were nicknamed "Wrens"

of the war had been preserved. The Germans had no inkling that Winston Churchill was privy to their secret messages.

THE BREAKTHROUGH THAT DID NOT SAVE COVENTRY—but did help win the war and played a crucial role on D-day—had its roots in Poland in the 1930s. Fearing Hitler's intentions, Polish intelligence agents bought a second-hand version of a coding machine developed by German inventor Arthur Scherbius in 1919, which had been commercially available until 1933, when the Nazis classified it as secret. Although the version of the Enigma machine used by the German military was much improved over the commercial model, the original provided some clues as to how Enigma might be broken. When Poland was overrun by the Nazis in 1939, the intelligence service smuggled the Enigma machine into England.

Enter Alfred Dilwyn Knox, an early scientific leader of the Ultra team, as the Bletchley Park codebreakers were known. Collaborating with Cambridge mathematician Alan Turing , Knox used the Polish sample of Enigma to build a decoding device nicknamed "the bombe." A primitive mechanical computer, it randomly tried every possible combination of letters in an intercepted message, based on an educated guess about a single word in the text, to try and break the code.

Knox and Turing made slow progress at first, but they were aided by some

German missteps. Central to Enigma's operation was the daily reconfiguration of its code. If it was reset each day using a random, three-letter sequence, its code would have been almost impossible to break. But some German operators simply set the machine's alphabetic gears on AAA or XYZ and left them there for the duration of the war. Moreover, the machine would never encode a letter as itself (thus, A would never stand for A), and it would always transpose the same letters for each other within a single message (for example, if A stood for B, then B had to stand for A).

Artifact

Enigma Machine

An early electric typewriter, the Enigma machine translated one letter into another by routing the electric current from each touch of the keypad (A, for example) through a series of plugs and rotors, which were set by the operator to convert them into the day's translation key. A small light would then come on next to a different letter (indicating, for example, that A should become P). The text of the message, now mere gibberish, was sent over telegraph lines or via radio (using Morse code) to an operator with another Enigma machine, using the same translation key to decode it.

These two predictable features reduced the staggeringly large number of possibilities the Bletchley Park team had to sort through. Luck also played a role: in May 1941, a German U-boat was captured off the coast of Greenland. Before the German crew could scuttle their craft, a British officer jumped aboard and retrieved one of the latest Enigma models, along with several code books.

Although the bombes developed at Bletchley Park were useful in breaking Enigma, they utilized a time-consuming, brute-force approach that simply tried every possible combination of letters until a coded message began to make sense. The next step was to create a machine that could make intelligent guesses and test them on its own, looking for recognizable patterns rather than random strings of text. To do the job, Turing built Colossus. One of the world's first binary computers, it took up several rooms and used more than 1,500 vacuum tubes. Turing's Colossus could break Enigma code in a fraction of the time required by the bombe.

Colossus began working on June 1, 1944, just in time for D-day. The dividends paid by real-time decryption of German radio traffic were immense. Prior to the invasion, Enigma intercepts provided accurate information about the location and status of all but two of the 58 German fighting units in the Normandy area. A final, delicious irony: on D-day itself, Allied commanders sometimes received word of their troops' progress faster through Enigma decrypts than through their own—understandably fragile—chains of command. At 7:35 a.m., the following message was decoded, "Five tanks ashore near Asnelles; English artillery firing inland, suspected landing near Ver-sur-Mer." Another message, at 8:25 a.m., read, "Arromanches-Bayeux road shelled; 35 tanks near Asnelles; further landings; Longues being shelled." The Enigma machine proved to be one of the most potent weapons of World War II—for both sides. ■

SHARDS: A service goes on amid the ruins of Coventry cathedral in 1940. Churchill knew of the attack, thanks to the breaking of the Enigma code, but he could not sound an alarm

COVENTRY, 1940

HANS WILD—TIME LIFE PICTURES

Father of a Binary Age

Cambridge University has always been a hothouse for eccentrics. But even there, Alan Turing stood out. On spring afternoons, the young don would ride his bicycle through the countryside while wearing a military-issue gas mask (to fend off pollen), with an alarm clock tied to his belt (to warn him when it was time to return to the classroom). But this absent-minded professor was far more brilliant than he was bizarre. In 1937 he published a paper that not only predicted the emergence of digital computers but also described how to build one.

Alan Mathison Turing was born in London in 1912. His father was a member of the British civil service in India; Alan and brother John spent their childhood in foster households in England, separated from their parents except for occasional visits. At 13, Alan enrolled at the Sherbourne School in Dorset and there showed a flair for mathematics. After twice failing to win a fellowship at the Cambridge's Trinity College, Turing received a fellowship from King's College, where he remained as a tutor after his graduation. And there he might happily have stayed, pondering theorems, had World War II not intervened.

The day after England entered the war against Germany in 1939, Turing was summoned to a Victorian mansion north of London. "Station X" (as Bletchley Park was code-named) would be the center of his life for the next six years. But this brilliant computer pioneer, whose war work involved codes and deceptions, had a secret of his own: he was homosexual in a society that scorned gays. In 1954, accused of a minor sexual offense, he killed himself by sucking on an orange he had injected with cyanide.

JUST AFTER 8 P.M. ON JUNE 6, ELEMENTS OF THE GERMAN 21st Panzer Division reached the village of Luc-sur-Mer, between Juno and Sword beaches on the Normandy coast. Twelve hours earlier, the veteran tank unit had been ideally positioned to drive a wedge between the Allied landings. It had been stationed less than two hours away from the British and Canadian invasion beaches, where, until the early afternoon of June 6, cloud cover was thick enough to prevent Allied fighters from attacking the tank columns as they advanced. What's more, during those hours, the British and Canadians had not yet landed enough men or heavy guns to repel a tank-driven assault. In all likelihood, a counterattack by these élite, well-equipped troops would have badly mauled the Allies landing at Juno and Sword. They might have pushed those troops back into the sea—which could have compromised Operation Overlord in its entirety.

But the order to activate the one German unit that could have seriously threatened the invasion was not given on the morning of June 6; it was not transmitted until 4 p.m., by which time the clouds had lifted, Allied aircraft were furiously strafing and bombing anything that moved on the German side of the lines, and the British and Canadian

JUNE 6, 1944

The Leaders

SITUATION REPORT Omaha Beach Les Moulins draw is opened; engineers begin clearing a route through Coleville draw ● Gold Beach British forces advance on Bayeux and take the road and rail lines linking it with Caen, but stop short of Caen itself and dig in for the night

"The news couldn't be better. As long as they were in Britain, we couldn't get at them. Now we have them where we can destroy them." —Adolf Hitler

REACTION: Late—too late—on D-day, Hitler studies a map of Normandy as Colonel General Alfred Jodl points out landing sites. German Foreign Minister Joachim von Ribbentrop is on far left. The news was so grave that Hitler forgot to take his reading glasses off for the photo

PARTING SHOT: Eisenhower denied Churchill's plea to take part in the landings, but Ike couldn't stop the Old Lion from crossing the Channel on June 12 to savor Overlord's success. After meeting with Allied top brass, Churchill reboarded the destroyer H.M.S. *Kelvin* and exulted as the ship fired its biggest guns at German artillery lairs inland

AMEN: On the radio, F.D.R. led Americans in a prayer for the soldiers

democracy and dictatorship was not confined to an abstract realm of ideas; it translated into a tactical advantage on the ground.

"They are landing here, and here," Hitler said to Luftwaffe boss Hermann Göring in a meeting at the dictator's Alpine retreat, Berchtesgaden, late in the afternoon. "Just where we expected them!" Normandy was, of course, exactly where the Germans were *not* expecting the Allied invasion to begin, but no one in Hitler's circle of intimates dared contradict him. Earlier in the afternoon, Hitler had struck a similarly surreal note at a diplomatic reception. "The news couldn't be better," he said. "As long as they were in Britain, we couldn't get at them. Now we have them where we can destroy them. It's begun at last."

Half a continent away, Joseph Stalin, the man whose entreaties, demands and threats had overridden Franklin D. Roosevelt's ambivalence and Winston Churchill's grave reservations to give the spark of life to Overlord, savored the news. Even after the Soviet army's battlefield victories over the Germans in 1943, Russia's situation was desperate. The new front in Western Europe promised to divert German men and arms away from the Eastern front. And it eliminated the possibility that England and America might make a separate peace with Germany—an option never considered in Washington or London but a nightmare in the paranoid imagination of the Soviet dictator. For Stalin, the end was at last in sight. He enthused several days after the invasion, "The history of war does not know of an undertaking comparable to it for breadth of conception, grandeur of scale and mastery of execution."

In London, Churchill stepped into the well in the House of Commons. The Prime Minister, haunted by Dunkirk, had initially been deeply skeptical about the wisdom of a frontal assault against Fortress Europe. Now he managed to contain his delight—briefly. For fifteen minutes he drove the backbenchers to distraction by discussing a different Allied victory, the capture of Rome two days earlier. But finally, as if it were an afterthought, he turned to more recent news: "I have also to announce to the House that during the night and early hours of the morning, the first of a series of landings in force upon the European continent has taken place. So far, commanders report that everything is proceeding according to plan. And what a plan!"

In Washington, President Roosevelt addressed the nation for the second time in 24 hours. Before asking listeners to join him in prayer, Roosevelt admitted what he had previously kept secret: "Last night when I spoke with you about the fall of Rome, I knew at that moment that troops of the United States and our Allies were crossing the Channel in another and greater operation. It has come to pass with success thus far."

Refracted in the historic prism of the great invasion, the war leaders' most telling traits were illuminated: Churchill the sly master of Parliament; F.D.R. his nation's father figure; Stalin a doubting, paranoid schemer; and Hitler, secluded in the Alps, a delusional, unchecked dictator. ∎

invasion troops had enough men and artillery on the beaches to fend off a thrust by any German units that approached. The reason for this fateful delay was that there was only one man in all of occupied Europe who could give such an order. And he was sleeping late.

Adolf Hitler began D-day tardily because he had taken sleeping pills late the night before and left orders not to be disturbed. So he didn't learn of the western front's turning point until he awoke, around noon. For several hours after, Hitler clung to the fantasy (already dismissed by senior officers on the scene, like General Gerd von Rundstedt) that the Normandy landings were a diversionary feint, meant to distract the Germans from a real invasion yet to come. By late afternoon, as the vast number of Allied troops in the landings proved that this was no sideshow, Hitler at last relented and ordered the panzer units into action.

The fact that it took a personal order from Hitler to move an individual unit underscores a fundamental difference between the Allied and German chains of command. While officers as junior as lieutenants and captains were taking the initiative on the Normandy beachheads, encouraged to improvise when necessary, the most senior officers in the German army were hamstrung: Hitler's mania for personal control meant that they could not make even minor tactical moves without his say-so. Von Rundstedt had hoped to drive his tanks into the gap between the British and Canadians as early as 8 a.m. but had been overruled. On D-day the divide between

BUNKER BRAVADO: Planners review blueprints for the Storey's Gate complex. Churchill put up a sign in the underground hideout quoting Queen Victoria on the Boer War: "Please understand there is no depression in this house and we are not interested in the possibilities of defeat; they do not exist"

The Secret Bunker of Mr. Churchill

This is the room from which I shall lead the war," Winston Churchill is said to have declared in May 1940, when he first inspected a complex of former storage spaces in the basement of London's Office of Works building, located 50 feet below street level, just steps from both the Prime Minister's residence at 10 Downing Street and the Houses of Parliament.

The Cabinet War Rooms were initially meant to serve as a bomb shelter. The original structure was reinforced with massive slabs of concrete and V-shaped cross beams, like those found inside the hull of a ship, which were designed to withstand the impact of 500-lb. bombs (at the war's outset); in 1944 they were reinforced to endure the power of a 1,700-lb. bomb, after the Germans began using V-2 rockets against London. When a bomb landed a few hundred yards from the complex in October 1940, Churchill casually remarked, "Pity it wasn't a bit nearer so that we might have tested our defenses."

Even after the Battle of Britain ended, the Cabinet War Rooms endured as Churchill's secret London redoubt. It was here that the Prime Minister and his inner circle would confer with senior military leaders, and it was from this bunker that Churchill spoke regularly to President Franklin Roosevelt through a special scrambler telephone developed by AT&T and installed in the complex shortly after the war began.

An entourage of more than 100 politicians, generals and spymasters—plus assorted clerks and cooks—attended Churchill, who ran morning staff meetings from his bed (which was modified to accommodate his girth) while smoking a cigar. (Following his afternoon nap, Churchill ran another meeting from his bathtub.) The staff worked in three shifts, and the lights in the complex burned steadily until the Japanese surrender in August 1945.

The complex, which Churchill and his staff referred to as Storey's Gate, or the Annex, was continually expanded throughout the war, eventually growing to hold cramped emergency sleeping quarters for more than 270 staff. An air filtration system (to guard against a possible gas attack by the Germans) was added to ready the catacomb as the site to which Churchill's entire government could retreat in a grave emergency. However, one modern convenience—up-to-date plumbing—was never installed; water was pumped in by hand, and everyone (Churchill included) made do with chamber pots, rather than toilets.

After years of neglect, portions of the Cabinet War Rooms were restored and opened to the public in the mid-1980s; the fully restored bunker is projected to open to visitors in 2005.

2100-2200 Hours

The Journalists

SITUATION REPORT Omaha Beach British forces arrive at Landing Zone W, west of the Orne River. The sight of their arrival, in more than 100 gliders, causes panic among the German armored troops of the 21st Panzer Division, leading to its withdrawal from the salient at Luc sur Mer to high ground near Caen ● **Juno Beach** Canadian landing troops moving toward Caen are halted by stiff German resistance, causing the Canadians to halt their advance

BY NIGHTFALL OF D-DAY, SOME OF THE JOURNALISTS who had witnessed the landings firsthand were already back in England, typing up stories, handing over film or delivering breathless eyewitness accounts into radio microphones. The scene in London was captured by Edward R. Murrow, CBS Radio's top European correspondent, whose voice was now an old friend to almost every American. "Reporters come in fresh from planes and landing craft, the dust of Normandy still on them ... There are no filing cabinets down here, no desks, just a long table ringed with typewriters. There aren't enough chairs. It's a triumph of cooperation between the American networks that

no man has yet been forced to write his copy standing up." The "down here" he referred to was a small, windowless, ill-ventilated cubbyhole deep in the basement of Britain's massive Ministry of Information. D-day "was U.S. radio's biggest moment, and radio did a job," said TIME's approving Press writer, who continued, "Listeners lucky enough to be awake through the first night of broadcasting had an experience they will remember to their graves. Into their living rooms came the voices of history: General Eisenhower and his supporting actors in the great drama; then, before dawn broke over the Eastern U.S., the first eyewitness reports by U.S. correspondents fresh back from the fighting."

"If your pictures aren't good enough, you aren't close enough."

—Robert Capa

Radio was the era's most immediate form of journalism, and a new advance—the portable tape recorder—caught the sounds of D-day with a vividness never experienced before. A BBC tape caught a bargeload of British tommies singing *For Me and My Gal* on their way to Normandy. NBC's Wright Bryan described the last minutes before a parachute jump brilliantly, then fell silent; listeners shivered to the fateful clicks as the troopers hooked up their automatic release belts.

Great events spark great journalism, and the names of those who covered World War II make up a Hall of Fame of reporting: Murrow, Walter Cronkite and Eric Sevareid on the radio; A.J. Liebling, Martha Gellhorn, James Agee and William L. Shirer in print. And it's impossible to visualize the war without thinking of the immortal footsoldiers Willie and Joe, drawn by the brilliant *Stars and Stripes* cartoonist Private Bill Mauldin.

Like Mauldin, newspaper columnist Ernie Pyle got down in the ditches with the regular troops, ate his share of K rations, confessed he was scared to death half the time and managed to limn the life of the average soldier in unequaled

War Scribes

FIRST MAN BACK: The photos of Bert Brandt, left, were pooled by the military, foiling his historic scoop. But he won bragging rights

COMRADES: "Papa," in a U.S. Army uniform, reads dispatches with the noted *New Yorker* writer Janet Flanner after the liberation of Paris in August

Bert Brandt

After the Normandy landings, photographers raced back to England with their photos. The winner: Acme's Bert Brandt. Taking no chance on couriers, he made three hitchhiking boat transfers in the middle of the Channel, reached England and finished his journey in a jeep.

The quest for scoops yielded some funny moments. LIFE photographer David Scherman told of arriving back in England, fresh from the beaches. He took up a post on his ship's lower deck, "so I could shoot the loading master signaling to us from the wharf and the immediate mad activity that I was sure would attend our arrival. The bow doors started groaning open and I waited with camera poised for the historic picture of whoever was outside. There was one person standing there—a swarthy character with a two-day beard, expectantly focusing his camera for the historic picture of whatever emerged from the slowly opening bow doors. He was LIFE's Robert Capa."

Ernest Hemingway

The famed novelist was as inflamed by the sound of the guns as his beloved bulls were by the matador's cape. Eager to see action, Hemingway found a billet as a war correspondent for *Collier's* magazine. He landed on Omaha Beach in the seventh wave; as supporting fire from the battleship U.S.S. *Texas* passed over his boat, Hemingway wrote, "Those troops who were not wax-grey with seasickness were watching the *Texas* with looks of surprise and happiness. Under the steel helmets they looked like pikemen of the Middle Ages to whose aid in battle had suddenly come some strange and unbelievable monster." But Hemingway's war work was hampered by his fame. Historian Stephen Ambrose railed at the novelist for his vanity and self-centeredness, contrasting "Papa" unfavorably with Ernie Pyle, who ate, slept and suffered with the average soldiers. Hemingway's best moment in the war was a triumph of self-mythologizing: he "liberated" the Ritz Hotel the day the Allies entered Paris and placed himself in charge of the wine-cellar detail.

fashion. His column ran six days a week in 310 newspapers across the U.S.; readers prayed for him, wrote to him, called their hometown newspapers to ask about his health and safety. Due to a foul-up, Pyle missed D-day; he landed on June 7. A few weeks later, Pyle made a surprising appearance on TIME's cover, then seemingly reserved for admirals and generals. In the cover story, a TIME writer told of catching up with Pyle in Normandy, "on the afternoon Cherbourg fell, and the fighting was still pretty hot ... I watched his face as he went down the street and he was scared all right. A little later we got mixed up in a tank-v.-pillbox duel and the pillbox knocked the tank out right outside of the house where we were. I said, 'Let's get out of here,' and Ernie said, 'O.K., you get a start and then I'll follow you.' I ran about 25 yards, didn't see Ernie, and

stopped in another house. When he reached me, he said: 'Some of those fellows that jumped out of that tank knew me from my picture so I had to stop and talk.'" Everybody, it seemed, knew Ernie.

TIME's story noted that as of mid-July, Pyle was about to return to the front—and was dreading it. "The thought of it gives me the willies," he said. "I have begun to feel I have about used up my chances." He survived the Battle of Normandy, only to die far away: Ernie Pyle was killed by a sniper's bullet on April 18, 1945, covering U.S. Marines on the island of Ie Shima in the Pacific theater. He is buried at the U.S. memorial cemetery near Pearl Harbor; at his request, his grave lies between that of two unknown soldiers.

Filmmakers and photographers did not fare as well as print

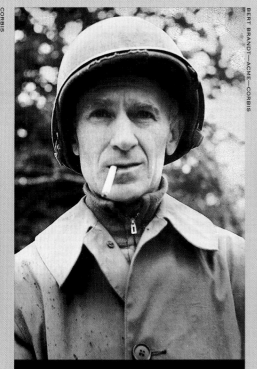

ONE OF THE GUYS: G.I.s universally loved Pyle, who shared their hardships and joys

A DAY AT THE OFFICE: TIME's Walton may have been the first journalist on the ground—or, as he explained, close to the ground

Ernie Pyle

The war's most famous reporter appeared on TIME's cover five weeks after D-day. The magazine quoted John Steinbeck on Pyle's gifts: "There are really two wars and they haven't much to do with each other. There is the war of maps and logistics, of campaigns, of ballistics, armies, divisions and regiments—that is General Marshall's war. Then there is the war of homesick, weary, funny, violent, common men who wash their socks in their helmets, whistle at girls and lug themselves through as dirty a business as the world has ever seen and do it with humor and dignity and courage—and that is Ernie Pyle's war."

William Walton

TIME correspondent Walton, a qualified parachutist, jumped into Normandy early June 6 with the U.S. 82nd Airborne Division. His landing, as he cabled TIME, was all too typical: "I plunged out of the plane door, happy to be leaving a ship that was heading toward flak and more Germans. The jump was from such low altitude there was only a moment to look around in the moonlight after my chute opened. The fields looked so small that one couldn't miss a tree or hedge. Anyway I couldn't. I landed in a pear tree—a rather good shock absorber. But the trouble was I didn't filter on through to the ground ... instead I dangled about three feet above ground ... My chute harness slipped up around my neck in a stranglehold, covering the knife in my breast pocket.

"I was helpless, a perfect target for snipers and I could hear some of them not far away. In a hoarse, frightened voice I kept whispering the password, hoping someone would hear and help. From a nearby hedge I heard voices. I hung still a moment, breathless. Then I heard therm more clearly. Never has a Middle Western accent sounded better. I called a little louder. Quietly Sergeant Auge, a fellow I knew, crept out of the hedge, tugged at the branches and with his pigsticker cut my suspension cords. I dropped like an overripe pear."

and radio journalists on D-day; the visual record of this historic event is far thinner than for other memorable battles of the war. Most of Robert Capa's photographs were ruined. The U.S. Army engaged the veteran Hollywood director John Ford to film the Overlord landings, and Ford and a camera team shot a good deal of footage. But when their work reached the U.S., it was deemed to be far too graphic for American audiences; only brief snippets of Ford's documentary record were ever seen in newsreels. Incredibly, almost all Ford's historic work was lost until 1998, when Melvin R. Paisley, a World War II aviator and Reagan-era Assistant Secretary of the Navy, found a few canisters of the missing film deep within the National Archives. Collaborating with director Steven Spielberg, actor Tom Hanks and TIME movie critic Richard Schickel,

Paisley created *Shooting War*, a 90-min. documentary saluting the filmmakers of World War II, which includes harrowing footage by cameraman Dick Taylor of American troops being mowed down on Omaha Beach.

The U.S. military was perhaps overcautious in censoring images it found too morbid for the public during the war. But in the conflict that Studs Terkel called "the Good War"—when there was little question as to the morality of the Allied cause—the relationship between the military and what we now call "the media" was relatively open and accommodating. Long before political imagemakers came up with the notion of "embedding" reporters with troops, the journalists in Normandy were proving that when it comes to war coverage, there's no substitute for sharing a foxhole with a soldier. ∎

Robert Capa

Born André Friedmann in Hungary, the photographer and his girlfriend Gerda Taro cooked up the alias "Robert Capa" as a sort of brand name, the better to sell their images to European photo agencies. Capa helped invent the notion of the combat photographer with his classic pictures of the Spanish Civil War, in which Taro was killed. Dashing and brave, Capa was already a legend when he landed on Omaha Beach at H-hour with the first wave of troops. His eyewitness account reflects his carefully cultivated persona—understated detachment from the horrific events he recorded:

"Just before 6 o'clock we were lowered in our LCVP and we started for the beach. It was rough and some of the boys were politely puking into paper bags.

I always said this was a civilized invasion. We heard something popping around our boat but nobody paid any attention. We got out of the boat and started wading and then I saw men falling and had to push past their bodies. I said to myself, 'This is not so good.' I was going in very elegant with my raincoat on my left arm, but at that moment, I had a feeling I would not need the raincoat. I let go of it and hid behind some tanks that were firing on the beach. After 20 minutes I suddenly realized that the tanks were a certain amount of cover from small-arms fire but that they were what the Germans were shooting shells at, so I made for the beach … It was very unpleasant there and having nothing else to do I started shooting pictures … "

Regan reflects at Omaha Beach in 1984

RENE BURRI—MAGNUM PHOTOS

The Man in the Picture

Robert Capa shot all his film at Omaha Beach, then made his way back to England on a medical craft to deliver it. But an overeager assistant in the LIFE picture bureau in London, rushing to see the shots, overheated the film, spoiling 98 of Capa's 106 images. The guilty assistant was Larry Burrows, who later became a great combat photographer in his own right; his pictures of the war in Vietnam are classics. Capa died in the field, after stepping on a mine in Indochina in 1954, while the French were fighting the Viet Minh. Burrows also died in Vietnam, when his helicopter crashed in 1971.

Shot in haste, with enemy fire shaking the camera, all of Capa's images of that dread morning are blurry. He was outraged when he finally saw his images in LIFE; far from the scene, an editor explained the shaky shots by saying the "immense excitement of [the] moment made Photographer Capa move his camera and blur [the] picture." Only later did Capa (like generations of viewers) realize that the blurriness of the images captures the intensity of the events.

Of Capa's pictures, the shot of a U.S. soldier edging his way through the water toward Omaha Beach is the most memorable; the G.I. seems to stand for all the unknown, brave men of D-day. But the man in the picture is no longer unknown. His mother had recognized him in 1944: he was Ed Regan, a private first class with the U.S. 116th Regiment, 29th Division. "For 35 years I never told anyone about it," said Regan. In 1982, the retired welfare program officer in Atlanta contacted LIFE, hoping to replace his only copy of the shot, a tattered, 38-year-old page from the magazine. The humble Regan was surprised at the response; he received a custom print of the picture from photographer Cornell Capa, brother of Robert, and was invited to New York City to attend a Liberation of France exhibition at the International Center of Photography. Recalling D-day, Regan said he was dead tired when the picture was taken: "I thought I could not go any further." But like his fellow soldiers, he did.

ROBERT CAPA—MAGNUM PHOTOS

EXTRA BONDS
TODAY !

CY'S BOND BO
eet Floor - B'way Bl
D. A. DEP
rth Floor

2200-2300 Hours

The Reaction

SITUATION REPORT **Omaha Beach** American forces have taken possession of several stone buildings at the western edge of Vierville and assumed defensive positions; other units advancing inland have surrounded the the town of St. Laurent on the east, south, and west • **Gold Beach** Advancing British forces reach the village of St. Aubin-d'Arquenay • **Aerial Bombardment** The second major bombing raid against St.-Lo commences

"The invasion? What about the invasion? Why hasn't someone told me?" —Mrs. Dwight D. Eisenhower

MOST AMERICANS WERE FAST ASLEEP AS ALLIED TROOPS WADED, SWAM AND stumbled onto the beaches of Normandy. As TIME reported, "Over the quiet American cities and the somnolent farms a bombers' moon shone through the cool June night. At 12:37 a.m. E.W.T. [Eastern war time, equivalent to daylight saving time], bells tinkled on the news tickers in newspapers and radio offices. FLASH: GERMAN TRANS-OCEAN AGENCY CLAIMS ALLIED INVASION HAS BEGUN. Out went the news over U.S. radio stations. Was this it? For three hours, Radio Berlin kept it up: paratroopers landed near the Seine estuary; the harbor of Le Havre shelled; Calais and Dunkirk raided by strong bomber formations. Every new flash brought the probability nearer. But most of the U.S. slept on.

"Finally the break came. The Allied side was going to speak. All four major networks stood by for London. Over the shortwave at last came the dry, deliberate voice of Colonel R. Ernest Dupuy, press aide to General Eisenhower: 'This is Supreme Headquarters, Allied Expeditionary Force. The text of Communiqué No. 1 will be released to the press and radio of the United Nations in 10 seconds.'

"In measured tones, Colonel Dupuy counted up to 10. Then, reading slowly, he confirmed the news: the invasion had begun, on the northern coast of France. For

"THIS JUST IN": A war-bond announcer in the window of Macy's department store in New York City reads bulletins from the front, as watchers crowd around

Angelenos get the news at the corner of Hollywood and Vine

Workers take a moment to pray in a Chicago manufacturing plant

Mom and Dad keep up at a California trailer camp

London office boys follow the news on ticker tape

the next few hours, the great, pulse-beating job of telling the U.S. people of the greatest military undertaking in history belonged to the U.S. radio. The U.S. slept on, but the radio worked as if it had the biggest audience in history. First, from London, came the rolling, authoritative voice of General Eisenhower, reading his proclamation to the people of Western Europe.

"Just an hour after Communiqué No. 1 came the first eye-witness account. NBC's Wright Bryan, who had flown over the invasion coast with paratroopers, stepped to a London microphone, breathlessly told of the lack of German opposition.

"At 3:30 a.m. in Marietta, Ga., the bell of the Methodist Church began to peal; by 4, every church was lighted, and in every church the people prayed. As morning came and the re-

alization finally dawned that this was D-day, across the land, generally, the mood was solemn. There was no sudden fear, as on that September morning in 1939 when the Germans marched into Poland, no sudden hate, as on Pearl Harbor day. This time, moved by a common impulse, the casual church-goers as well as the devout went to pray.

"The U.S. people had wondered for weeks how they would behave on D-day. When it came, they went about their regular business. Race tracks called off their programs for the day; many stores closed at noon. The citizens struck to their radios, read newspaper extras as they rolled off the presses, sat and thought, stood and drank, knelt and prayed. Awakened by a New York *Post* reporter at her West Point hotel, Mrs. Dwight

Newspaper vendors do brisk business in Chicago on the long-awaited day

Taking in F.D.R.'s speech at La Guardia airfield

Farmworkers take five in California

Elders sound the shofar at the Brooklyn (N.Y.) Hebrew Home

Eisenhower exclaimed: 'The invasion? What about the invasion? Why hasn't someone told me?'

"Londoners acted like good Englishmen. U.S. newspaper correspondents rushed to Piccadilly Circus, hoping to see something like Times Square on New Year's Eve. They found Londoners going to work as usual. When the news reached Lyons, France, thousands on their way to work hugged and kissed in Gallic joy, sang *La Marseillaise*, shouted '*Vive la France! Vive les Allies!*'

"In Moscow, the people literally danced in the streets. There the populace, from Stalin down to the lowest party member, had waited for two and a half years for the Second Front. This was the happiest capital. The Russian radio called it "The Victory Front." In the lobby of the Metropole Hotel, an ecstatic Muscovite threw her arms around an American correspondent, exclaimed, 'We love you, we love you, we love you. You are our real friends.'" ∎

Artifact

Complimentary Issue

A t right, Lieut. D.E. Condon, of Goshen, Va., at his airfield in England, replies to the TIME magazine circulation office, which sent him a free issue of the magazine, along with a routine form letter inviting Condon to subscribe so he could keep up with the war news from the front lines. The day he received the issue, Condon had just returned from spending four hours in the skies over France, directing the Allied bombardment of Cherbourg.

A FEW MINUTES BEFORE MIDNIGHT ON JUNE 6, General Erwin Rommel arrived at his French field headquarters in La Roche-Guyon, after a day-long drive from Germany, where he had gone to visit his family, believing no Allied invasion was imminent. A hasty briefing from his staff left the German commander with little reason to be encouraged. The most immediate bad news was that a counterattack against British positions by the 21st Panzer Division had failed. Hours earlier, Rommel had stopped at a communications station and ordered this thrust. At the time, he had exclaimed to his aide, Captain Hellmuth Lang, that "if the 21st Panzer can make it, we might just be able to drive them back in three days." The chances of this were better than even Rommel knew. In a major intelligence failure, Allied planners had failed to follow up on signs of the unit's presence in Normandy, only miles from the British landing grounds. If this tank detachment, the only fully mobile German army division within striking distance of the invasion beaches, could

pin down the British forces on Juno and Sword beaches, the entire eastern flank of Operation Overlord would be made vulnerable to subsequent attacks by slower German units, positioned farther to the rear. As one of the 21st Panzer's commanders, Colonel Hermann von Oppeln-Bronikowski, had been told just before his advance, "The future of Germany may very well rest of your shoulders. If you don't push the British back into the sea, we've lost the war."

But even this, Rommel's single best chance to contain the Allies on the beaches, was stillborn. The order for the 21st Panzer Division to drive for the coast came too late, as Rommel himself seemed to sense. Back in his car a few minutes after issuing the directive, he said to Lang: "If I was the commander of the Allied forces right now, I could finish off the war in 14 days."

In the event, a furious assault by the British 3rd Division and withering fire from Allied fighter planes stopped the tanks of the 21st Panzer Division in their tracks. Shortly

2300-2400 Hours

Digging In

SITUATION REPORT **Operation Overlord** More than 175,000 Allied troops have landed in France. Few units have achieved their objectives, but none have been repelled. As Allied forces assume defensive positions for the night, the Germans consolidate their forces in the city of Caen • **The Enemy** German forces are deployed in line with Rommel's strategy of confining the Allied troops to the beachhead. By pressing close to the enemy's lines, the Germans hope to restrict Allied air strikes, while preparing for an armored counterattack that will push the invaders back into the sea

after 2300, Von Oppeln-Bronikowski ordered his unit to take a defensive stance: "Tanks to be dug in. Position must be held." At almost the same moment, nearly the same instructions—to dig in and hold your position—were going out to practically every Allied unit on French soil. And if Erwin Rommel had known exactly where those units were located, and in what numbers, he might have cut his estimate of 14 days in half.

In England, General Dwight Eisenhower had a more complete picture of the situation than did Rommel—and more basis for optimism. Across all five invasion beaches, Allied troops had gained a toehold. The news was best from Utah Beach, where many of the U.S. 4th Division's objectives (notably the capture of the four western exits from the Normandy beachheads) had been achieved. Troops of the 4th Division had moved as far as six miles inland and had linked up with paratroopers who had been dropped near Ste.-Mère-Église, all at a cost of fewer than 20 dead and 200 wounded.

From Gold Beach, the reports were nearly as encouraging.

Although British troops had not taken Bayeux or managed to cut the road linking it with Caen, they had reached Arromanches and were preparing for the arrival of sections of the artificial Mulberry harbors the following morning, promising to accelerate the scheduled influx of men and supplies.

At Juno Beach, the Canadians had not achieved the objective of taking the Caen-Bayeux road, nor had they linked up with British forces moving off Sword Beach. But the Canadians had moved inland quickly from their landing beaches and were positioned close to their objectives. At Sword, the good news in part consisted of what not had happened: the 21st Panzer Division had failed to drive a wedge between the

TAKING COMMAND: Forty-eight hours before, Omaha Beach was a chaotic, bloody battlefield; now it has been transformed into a gigantic Allied supply terminal, as ships speed men, vehicles and matériel into France

JUNE 8, 1944

"If I was the commander of the Allied forces right now, I could finish off the war in 14 days."

—General Erwin Rommel

troops coming off Sword Beach and those coming off Juno. But though commandos had moved off Sword to link up with British airborne units and hold two key bridges inland, the optimistic goal of taking Caen on D-day had not been reached.

The bulletins from Omaha Beach were the most sobering. The landing site for two-thirds of all U.S. invasion troops on D-day had also been the scene of more than 90% of the American casualties. But what had appeared at one early point to be a potential disaster had been salvaged by the courage and determination of troops from the U.S. 29th Division. By midnight, the Allies held Omaha and had reached as deep as 1½ miles inland in the area of Coleville.

As information about the Allied airborne troops positioned behind the beaches trickled into SHAEF headquarters, the emerging picture was a similarly confusing jigsaw puzzle, but there was as at least as much good news as bad. The U.S. 101st Airborne Division had accomplished the most important of its D-day missions, securing the western and southern flanks of Allied troops moving in from the beaches. Farther east, troops from the U.S. 82nd Airborne Division had linked up with 4th Division troops from Utah Beach, and together they held Ste.-Mère-Église. British airborne troops had held the bridges over the Caen Canal and Orne River until British landing forces from Sword Beach fought their way inland. And by D-day's end, hundreds more British gliders had touched down west of the Orne to reinforce this position.

One theme ran through all these dispatches, and it was both puzzling and exhilarating to Eisenhower and his staff: the aggressive German tactics that Overlord troops had been told to expect (and Overlord planners most feared) were not in evidence. Even in areas like Omaha Beach, where German troops were well equipped and present in large numbers, they limited themselves to a stubborn defense, rather than taking the offensive and trying to repel the invasion.

By midnight, more than 156,000 Allied troops had crossed the beaches. Another 19,000 Airborne troops had dropped from the sky. All told, they now claimed ownership over some 80 square miles of territory that had belonged to Adolf Hitler

Prisoners of War

Their ethos centered on racial purity, but the Nazis discovered the advantages of diversity once the war in Russia began depleting the ranks of the German army. One such compromise was the formation of *Ost* (East) battalions, which were populated by non-German nationals from more than a dozen Baltic and Slavic nations, as well as Russia, much of Asia and as far away as India. In many cases, *Ost* battalion soldiers (who could not rise above the rank of private and were always led by NCOs and ethnic German officers) would realize the overwhelming strength of the Allied landings, then happily shoot their German leaders and emerge from a bunker, smiling, with their hands in the air. Even German fighting units often consisted of young boys and old men. But any soldier wearing a German uniform surrendered at his own peril. Germans on the other side of the front line would often shoot such "traitors" as punishment for violating Hitler's order that not an inch of ground could be given up. Even so, by the end of the Battle of Normandy, more than 200,000 Germans would be prisoners of war and the Allies would be taking new prisoners at the rate of 30,000 a month.

FACE OF THE ENEMY: A U.S. soldier guards two German youngsters; they claimed their age was 18. The German units at Normandy were heavily stocked with aging and ailing troops, prisoners from the Eastern front and German teenagers

CHOW TIME: General Eisenhower enters a camouflaged mess tent while meeting Allied field commanders in Normandy the week after D-day. At far left is General Carl Spaatz of the Royal Air Force; Admiral Ernest King of the Royal Navy faces the camera

the day before. This foothold had not come cheaply: some 10,000 Allied troops had been killed or wounded in the first 24 hours of the landings. But there was consolation even in this grim statistic, for the casualties were far fewer than planners had expected as the price of invading France.

All over Normandy, Allied troops took what shelter they could find in barns, abandoned German bunkers and shell craters, then settled in for the night. General Omar Bradley would later write in his diary that as D-day drew to a close, Omaha Beach commander Charles Huebner "was impatient to clean up the beachhead that he might drive inland and secure his immediate objectives. 'It'll take time and ammunition,' I told him, 'perhaps more than we reckon on both.'"

At Rommel's headquarters, Captain Lang asked the general, "Sir, do you think we can drive them back?" Rommel shrugged and answered, "I hope we can. I've nearly always succeeded up to now." Then Rommel told Lang, "You look tired. Why don't you go to bed? It's been a long day." Outside, the bell from a nearby church sounded midnight. ∎

HOME: A German bunker is now headquarters for an Allied unit. Most bunkers were built so solidly that they didn't collapse, even if their inhabitants were killed. Above, German soldiers surrender to Allied troops

SEARCH PARTY: The clifftop dunes above some of the landing beaches were grassy, wind-swept highlands that provided cover for advancing U.S. troops on D-day—but also for German snipers in the days after the invasion

battle of normandy

Next Stop: Paris

The Allies move off the beaches but are held back by the hedgerows of Normandy until the huge tide of men and armor swamps the Germans

FOR EISENHOWER AND MONTGOMERY, FOR CHURCHILL, Roosevelt and Stalin, for millions of fighting men around the world wearing Allied uniforms—and for millions more whose hopes were pinned on their success—the morning of June 7 brought much cause to be gravely concerned but also many reasons to be thankful. Almost none of the invading troops who had landed the previous day had fully achieved the ambitious objectives set out for them in the Overlord plan. But those troops had clambered onto French soil and had not been pushed back into the sea. The tenuous foothold they had gained in German-occupied France was at no point more than a few miles deep, and in some places it extended only a few hundred yards from the shore. But the troops were dug in and ready to stab farther into

France, while new waves of tens of thousands more soldiers were flooding onto the beaches behind them, a rising tide of khaki and olive drab.

For Hitler, Rommel and Von Rundstedt, and for all whose fortunes were tied to Nazi conquest, the first light of dawn on June 7 brought with it many reasons to be apprehensive—and just one to be optimistic. Realists, such as Hitler's two commanding generals in Normandy, knew that if the Allies succeeded in establishing a secure beachhead, through which they could bring in large numbers of reinforcements and supplies, there was almost no hope of dislodging them. On the other side of the German Empire, at Hitler's mountain retreat in the Bavarian Alps, even the transfixed sycophants in the dictator's inner circle found the prospect of fighting a losing

"The enemy will succeed ... in breaking through our own meager front. The troops are fighting heroically everywhere, but the unequal struggle is coming to an end."

—General Erwin Rommel, to Hitler

war in Russia, another on the Italian peninsula and now a third in France disquieting. Yet the one reason the Germans had for optimism was formidable—and nature's handiwork.

The word that the French used to describe the Norman countryside, *bocage*, translates roughly as "box country." It refers to the checkerboard layout of thousands of small meadows and fields, each bounded by high earthen banks, topped with a tall line of thick, centuries-old hedges and traversed by narrow sunken lanes. The berms at the edge of each field make natural fortifications. The hedgerows form perfect camouflage in which troops, artillery pieces and tanks can dig in and hide. Each one of these thousands of fields of an acre

or less could be defended for days with relative ease, even against a numerically superior, better-supplied force. To advance just a single mile, a squad of Allied infantry would have to cross as many as 30 of these "boxes."

As for Normandy's low, winding roads, they seemed almost to have been designed to conduct ambushes against invaders. Limiting visibility and hampering maneuverability, they turned tanks and armored vehicles into clumsy, vulnerable behemoths. Infantrymen attempting to travel such a road on foot were surrounded by concealed high ground from which an enemy could pick them off at will. And when the enclosed fields, hedgerows and country lanes gave way to a clearing or

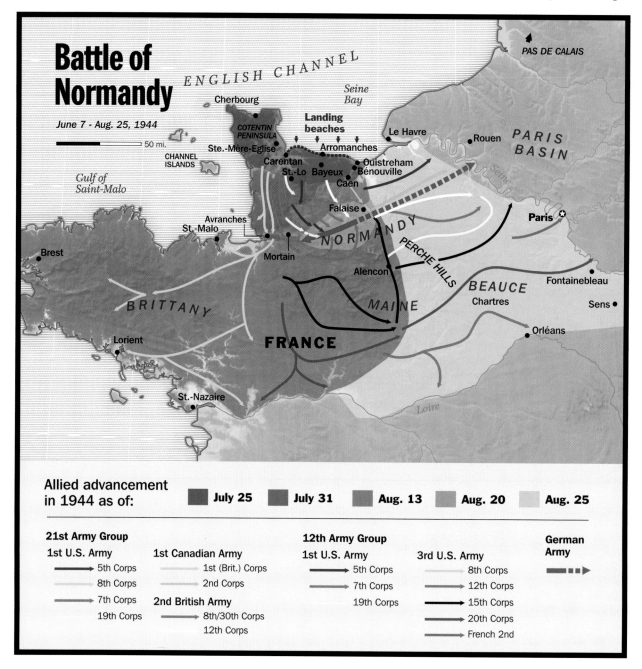

Battle of Normandy

June 7 - Aug. 25, 1944

50 mi.

Allied advancement in 1944 as of: ■ **July 25** ■ **July 31** ■ **Aug. 13** ■ **Aug. 20** ■ **Aug. 25**

21st Army Group

1st U.S. Army
→ 5th Corps
→ 8th Corps
→ 7th Corps
19th Corps

1st Canadian Army
→ 1st (Brit.) Corps
→ 2nd Corps

2nd British Army
→ 8th/30th Corps
12th Corps

12th Army Group

1st U.S. Army
→ 5th Corps
→ 7th Corps
19th Corps

3rd U.S. Army
→ 8th Corps
→ 12th Corps
→ 15th Corps
→ 20th Corps
→ French 2nd

German Army
■■■▶

FIRST PRIZE: U.S. soldiers relax in St.-Mére-Église, the first French town to fall to the Allies. Paratroopers were killed as they landed here early on June 6, while the city was burning from Allied bombs. More U.S. troops entered around 0430, and 30 Germans surrendered

a small village, many of the houses—indeed some whole towns—turned out to have been constructed in medieval times specifically to serve as fortresses against invaders.

It was this prospect that British Field Marshal Bernard Montgomery, who had taken part in the bloody, stalemated trench warfare of World War I, dreaded most. The supreme commander of Allied ground forces (and No. 2 to Eisenhower) was determined that Normandy's obstacles would have to be overcome by courage and ingenuity. An early instance of the former came from General Norman Cota, who had rallied U.S. troops on Omaha Beach on D-day. The next morning he came upon an infantry squad that had stopped its advance in front of a house near the beach. A young captain explained that "the Germans are in there, shooting at us." Cota told the captain and his men to fire on it, saying, "I'll show you how to take a house with Germans in it." As the infantry opened fire, Cota and a second squad ran toward it, screaming like madmen and tossing hand grenades through the windows. Cota then kicked open the front door, threw in more grenades and entered the house, firing his rifle. The few Germans who survived ran out the back door in a panic. "You've seen how to

take a house," Cota said to the infantry squad afterward. "Do you know how to do it now?"

Meanwhile, an example of fighting the terrain with ingenuity came from U.S. Major General J. Lawton (Lightning Joe) Collins: his riposte to the *bocage* was the "rhinoceros"—a Sherman tank with rails taken from Rommel's beach obstacles welded onto the front, forming a giant set of garden shears that could uproot hedgerows as the tank plowed through.

O N JUNE 7, AS MONTGOMERY CAME ASHORE IN NORMANDY and Rommel had just returned to France from a holiday in Germany, the first order of business for Allied invasion troops was to close all the gaps in their line, linking the five invasion beaches in a continuous front. For the most part, this meant advancing in a line parallel to the shore, rather than directly into German-held territory. But this advance did bring the first prize seized on D-day plus one, when the city of Bayeux was cleared of the last German resistance.

The next day, as the British 50th Division linked up with the U.S. 1st Division at Port-en-Bassin, northwest of Bayeux, the last significant hole in the Allied lines was closed. The invaders were now arrayed along a continuous front, 60 miles long. Momentum, however, seemed to be slipping from the Allies' grasp. Once the Germans realized they had lost the battle of the beaches, they rushed reinforcements to Caen, which commanded the high ground, contained the key Carpiquet airfield and controlled the roads to Paris. Montgomery had

BARRIERS: A U.S. antitank unit takes aim through a hedgerow at German armor in the countryside around Saveur-le-Vicomte. The Normandy landscape was as much an obstacle to the Allies as were the German troops, holding up the advance toward Paris for weeks

planned to capture Caen on D-day, but now the Germans were rebuffing every Allied foray, creating a stalemate.

At nearby Carentan, the news was better. Advancing U.S. troops from Omaha and Utah beaches encircled the city on June 10, linked up on its southern outskirts and forced Carentan to surrender two days later. This seems to have prompted Montgomery to attempt a similar pincer movement against Caen. But the Germans counterattacked, hurling élite, experienced divisions—the 1st SS Panzer Division, (Liebstandarte Adolf Hitler,) and the 2nd SS Panzer Division, (Das Reich)—into the battle, stalling the British drive and restoring the deadlock.

THE NEXT MORNING, FROM HIS FIELD HEADQUARTERS IN Rastenburg in East Prussia (the "Wolf's Lair"), Adolf Hitler made a fateful decision. Just as he had earlier hamstrung Rommel and Von Rundstedt by assuming exclusive authority over the most German important combat units, Hitler now decreed that under no circumstances could any German commander in France withdraw from Nazi-occupied territory. If a German unit was about to be massacred but could save itself (or even stop an Allied advance) by pulling back to a more defensible position, it nonetheless would have to stand fast and be slaughtered. At the same time, Hitler dispatched tank commander SS General Sepp Dietrich—a personal favorite and fanatical Nazi—to assume command of the German defenses in Caen.

By June 12, Montgomery had formed a new plan for laying siege to Caen. Instead of the direct frontal assault he had tried a few days earlier, he would instead use British and Canadian troops to take the nearby town of Villers-Bocage, which occupied a strategic crossroads southwest of the city and controlled access to it. The tragedy that ensued was testimony to the Germans' skill at using the natural defenses afforded by Normandy's terrain to their own advantage. As a large British column of tanks and other armored vehicles advanced on Villers-Bocage, it was forced to proceed down one of the sunken lanes that lined the hedgerows. German tanks were waiting on high ground, behind the walls of foliage. They remained silent until the entire Allied column was within point-blank range of the guns and then destroyed the lead British tank, blocking the rest of the column from further advance. Because the road was too narrow for any of the British vehicles to turn around, and backing out was impossible in the chaos of a close-quarters battle, the British had to stand and fight. Although they battled the Germans heroically, the British infantrymen were in an impossible situation. In the space of a few minutes, dozens were killed and more than 50 tanks and other armored vehicles were destroyed. As a result, the British failed to take Caen during this action, while the Germans reoccupied Villers-Bocage.

In England, both Eisenhower and Churchill were growing increasingly frustrated with the lack of progress at Caen. Later, Churchill would hint to Eisenhower that if he wanted to relieve a senior British commander, he could do so without fear of objection from the Prime Minister. But Montgomery had been heavily promoted to Britons and Americans alike as the can-do Rommel beater of the African campaign, and Eisenhower, though sorely tempted, decided that sacking "Monty" in the middle of a battle might upset the chain of command and damage Allied unity. He resolved instead to vis-

■ battle of normandy

it the British general's field headquarters and admonish him "to get on his bicycle."

From the remove of London, both Eisenhower and Churchill believed that Caen could easily have been sealed off and bypassed rather than overrun. But on the ground, Montgomery was formulating a new strategy. If he continued to threaten the city, he reasoned, the Germans would reinforce it, concentrating their limited resources in one place and creating the chance for a breakout elsewhere. In effect, Montgomery was passing the baton to American General Omar Bradley for a breakout on the western end of the Allied line, while he kept the Germans busy at Caen. This could not have been an easy decision for the proud British general: unable to take Caen on D-day, he had hoped, at the least, to lead the Allied breakout himself.

AS LATE AS JUNE 16, HITLER WAS HOLDING 250,000 TROOPS AND HUNDREDS OF tanks in reserve on the western front to meet the invasion he still believed would come at Pas de Calais; incredibly, he still thought that Overlord might not be the main Allied landing. When Rommel and Von Rundstedt protested that this was preposterous, Hitler flew to their rear-area headquarters in Soissons. Unmoved by his generals' pleas, Hitler refused their requests for more battlefield authority and ordered once again that no ground could be surrendered.

Then, on June 19, the worst storm the English Channel had seen in half a century began to rage over Normandy; it lasted for three days. One of the two artificial "Mulberry" harbors the invaders had built off the landing beaches was wrecked, and more than 800 Allied ships were sunk, beached or severely damaged. The timing of the storm raises two intriguing hypothetical questions. First, June 19 was the fallback date for the D-day landings, if June 6 proved impossible. What if the Allies had tried to invade France on this day? Almost without question, the invasion would have failed. Second, the Great Storm (as the British called it) momentarily gave the Germans a unique opportunity. With Allied air forces grounded and with

IMPERIAL WAR MUSEUM

The Full Monty

Bernard Law Montgomery, Britain's most famous warrior since Wellington, was the third son of an Anglican missionary and a domineering Victorian mother. Born in 1887, Montgomery spent much of his childhood in one of the remotest corners of the British Empire, Tasmania, at a time when the Aborigine population was being exterminated. After graduating from the Royal Military Academy, Sandhurst, in 1908, he earned a reputation as a brave and talented officer (he was wounded twice in World War I) but also as an outsider, an eccentric and a spartan warrior. Of his days at an English boarding school, he said that he had been "well beaten, and I am better for it." Modern warfare, he insisted, called for new blood, sharp minds and physically fit leaders. "I don't smoke," Montgomery once bragged, "don't drink, and I'm 100% fit!" Winston Churchill's rejoinder: "I smoke and I drink, and I'm 200% fit!"

"Monty" emphasized meticulous planning and rigorous training. The former tendency often drove his superiors, who suspected it was a pretext to avoid engaging the enemy, to distraction; the latter inspired the rank-and-file troops he commanded. He took a perverse delight in sharing unwelcome opinions with his superiors. Meeting with Churchill after Dunkirk, Montgomery appalled the Prime Minister by demanding that the entire British high command be sacked.

Defying British military tradition, Montgomery always lingered close to the front lines and demanded an unheard-of degree of logistical integration—qualities that helped him crush German General Erwin Rommel in North Africa. Of that victory, Churchill would later say, "Before Alamein we never had a victory; after Alamein we never had a defeat."

U.S. ARMY—AP/WIDE WORLD

FIRE! Three soldiers from a U.S. artillery brigade direct a howitzer at retreating Germans near Carentan, one of the first key towns to fall to Allied troops after D-day

supplies and reinforcements lagging because of the wrecked artificial harbor, a German counterattack might have turned the course of events. Sensing a critical juncture, Hitler ordered Rommel and Von Rundstedt to attack with five divisions within 24 hours. But it was typical of the fantasy world that Hitler had begun to inhabit that three of those divisions had not yet arrived in Normandy, and two of them were pinned down trying to hold the line against Allied advances. The counterattack that might have made a difference never came.

The opportunity would not come again. By the time the storm ended, the Allies had landed more than 557,000 troops, 81,000 vehicles and 183,000 tons of supplies on French soil. Thus fortified, on June 26 Montgomery launched Epsom, the first of three operations ostensibly designed to take Caen but actually intended at least as much to focus German attention and resources there.

On June 27, the day after Montgomery launched the feint, the port of Cherbourg fell to American troops of the U.S. VII Corps, commanded by Lightning Joe Collins. This was the first of the breakouts that Montgomery hoped his siege of Caen would facilitate. It was a turning point: Cherbourg's huge natural harbor, although expertly sabotaged by the departing Germans, soon more than made up for the loss of the Mulberry at Omaha and ratcheted up the feverish pace at which Allied troops and supplies now were landing.

Back at Caen, the British troops Montgomery deployed for Epsom faced three panzer divisions within the city, with another advancing nearby. Epsom's strategic objective was Hill 112, on the southern approach to Caen. From this commanding high ground, fire could be directed into the city and enemy movements observed for dozens of miles in every direction. During the four days that Epsom raged, the Germans and British exchanged possession of Hill 112 multiple times, with the attacker in each instance paying the defender an ever higher price in blood. The hill finally fell to the British, but little British advancement had been accomplished elsewhere.

On the invasion beaches and at Cherbourg, however, much had been achieved: the influx of Allied manpower and equipment was turning into a tidal wave. By June 30—only 10 days after the Great Storm and the day Montgomery called off Epsom—the invaders had landed an additional 320,000 troops,

RUINED: A lost prize that became a pawn in the bitter duel between Montgomery and German top general Gert von Runstedt, the city of Caen was laid waste in the long siege before it finally fell to the Allies in mid-July. The price of victory was the devastation of the historic city

■ battle of normandy

31,000 vehicles and 390,000 tons of supplies. These numbers ensured that the Allies could afford prolonged, meat-grinding stalemates like the one at Caen. The Germans, running short of men, armor, ammunition, gasoline and all other matériel essential to modern warfare, could not.

Within the German high command, Von Rundstedt was reaching the limits of his endurance. He cabled Hitler, demanding more supplies and reinforcements, as well as the authority to make tactical withdrawals if necessary. When senior generals in Berlin reached Von Rundstedt by telephone and asked for his recommendations, he sarcastically suggested that they open peace negotiations with the Allies. On July 2, Hitler declared that he had accepted Von Rundstedt's resignation. As if to celebrate, a day later the Allies launched the second forward thrust made possible by the siege of Caen, as General Bradley hurled an offensive against St.-Lo. But the foray ground to a halt after only minor gains, a victim of bad weather and fanatical German resistance. St.-Lo would not fall to the Allies until July 19.

THE SECOND OF MONTGOMERY'S TRIUMVIRATE OF OPERATIONS AGAINST CAEN, Operation Charnwood, began on July 8. The battle opened with a massive, devastating raid by British and American strategic bombers. Within two days, the Allies held the northern half of the city, including the vital Carpiquet airfield, another overly optimistic British D-day objective that had gone unachieved. This meant that Allied planes could now be based in large numbers on French soil, rather than flying round trip across the English Channel for each mission, dramatically increasing the reach and effectiveness of Allied air operations.

One measure of this increased effectiveness came a week later, on July 17, when a British fighter strafed Rommel's limousine. The general survived but was so seriously wounded that he had to relinquish his command of German forces in Normandy. A few days earlier he had written privately to Hitler that "the enemy will succeed in the foreseeable future in breaking though our own meager front, and break into broader French territory … The troops are fighting heroically everywhere, but the unequal struggle is coming to an end. I must ask you to accept the consequences of this situation." Hitler's reply was to issue for the third time his edict that not an inch of the Reich's territory would be conceded.

The response from Rommel and other officers, who now believed Hitler was dragging Germany over the edge of an abyss, came on July 20, when a bomb exploded in Hitler's Rastenburg headquarters. With what biographer Ian Kershaw called "the luck of the devil," Hitler survived. Within months, hundreds of senior army officers would be put to death in the ghastliest ways Hitler's secret police could devise. The lucky ones, Erwin Rommel among them, were allowed to commit suicide.

While the generals were trying without success to finish off Hitler, Montgomery was having considerably more success in finishing off the German resistance inside Caen. His third sally, Operation Goodwood, began on July 18 and concluded the same day that a staff officer's briefcase exploded under Hitler's map table. With Caen subdued and much of the troop strength the Germans had concentrated there now decimated, Montgomery could at last proceed as he had hoped to in the first 48 hours after D-day. On July 24, five days after U.S. forces under Bradley at last conquered St.-Lo, Montgomery sent the Americans driving westward toward Brittany. Simultaneously, Montgomery drove his elated, advancing units of British and Canadian infantry southward toward Falaise with 2,600 tanks.

Waiting to leap into the gap between Bradley's westward advance (Operation Cobra) and Montgomery's march south (a continuation of Operation Goodwood) was General George S. Patton. Much to his seething frustration, Patton had been kept in England for weeks after D-day, to preserve the illusion that he was in command of a huge task force that would soon land at Pas de Calais—the "real" invasion that Hitler had been tricked into expecting and for which he had held back his reserves, contributing greatly to the German disaster in Normandy. Now, new units that arrived in France at the end of July were folded into Patton's newly created Third Army.

Five miles into Montgomery's advance, he captured the railroad line between

BOB LANDRY—TIME LIFE PICTURES

The G.I.'s General

Desperately poor" was how Omar Bradley described the Clark, Mo., family he was born into in 1893. The son of a rural schoolteacher, he was orphaned at age 14 when the father he adored died of pneumonia from walking six miles to work each day through harsh, Midwest winters. Bradley knew from an early age that education would better his lot in life. As a teenager, working for 17¢ an hour on the Wabash Railroad, he tried to support his mother and two stepsisters and dreamed of saving enough to attend the University of Missouri. It was Bradley's Sunday school teacher who suggested that he apply to West Point. A natural gift for mathematics and logic helped Bradley gain admission and graduate 44th out of 164 cadets in 1915, the year that is remembered as "the class the stars fell on": 30 graduates would eventually serve as generals in World War II.

Bradley (at right above) never set foot on a battlefield until well into the war, at the advanced age of 50. In 1943 West Point classmate Dwight Eisenhower sent him to North Africa, where he helped rout the Germany army. Now viewed as a logistical and organizational genius, Bradley helped plan the invasion of Sicily, where he again led troops to victory. Ike soon named Bradley the commander of U.S. ground troops on D-day.

Amid a pantheon of American and British generals who actively fostered their own cults of personality, Bradley never lost the common touch. His humility and concern for the average soldier's lot earned him a reputation as "the G.I.'s general." War correspondent Ernie Pyle once wrote of Bradley, "I don't believe I have ever known a person to be so universally loved and respected by the men around and under him."

PAYBACK: Captain Earl Topley, who led one of the first American units into German-occupied Cherbourg, examines the body of a "last stand" German sniper who was reponsible for killing three of Topley's men

Caen and Paris. But then his troops encountered serious German resistance and again ground to a halt, leading to a stern rebuke from Eisenhower, who warned Montgomery that he would not tolerate a repeat of the delays at Caen. On the other end of the Allied front, the Americans were similarly bogged down, advancing only two miles in the first day of Operation Cobra. But then Bradley pushed two armored columns forward and punched a three-mile-wide gap in the German lines. By July 30, Avranches had been seized, opening the way to the Loire River and Brittany, with its valuable ports of St.-Malo and Brest. After six days, the Americans were rolling almost unopposed through open country—chasing German forces who were in headlong retreat and taking horrific casualties. Patton was exactly where he had wanted to be since leaving Italy in 1943—in command of the clattering armored vehicles that were leading the advance.

The situation now deteriorated for the Germans in two ways. First, as they moved out of fixed positions, they were forced to abandon telegraph lines and rely more on radio transmission. This played to the Allied ability to decrypt the Germans' Ultra code, tipping the U.S. and British commanders to German moves well in advance. The second problem was the Germans' slow pace. Although it is seldom remembered today (primarily because Nazi propaganda films rarely depicted this side of military life), most German infantry units were not motorized: they traveled in simple carts at a speed of one horsepower—two horsepower, if lucky. Germans traversing the *bocage* in open-topped wagons pulled by farm an-

imals were defenseless to attack from above. Entire regiments were cut to pieces by Allied fighter pilots—who often knew exactly where to look for them, thanks to "ultra" intercepts.

Now reduced to gambling, Hitler ordered Field Marshall Gunther von Kluge (Von Rundstedt's replacement) to direct his remaining forces in a counterattack against Avranches, hoping to isolate the Americans in Brittany and the Cotentin Peninsula. Von Kluge pointed out that success was unlikely, and the price of failure would be a surrounded German army. But Hitler insisted, and Von Kluge reluctantly obeyed.

On Aug. 6 the Germans began a 50-mile thrust westward, from the Falaise area toward Avranches on the Atlantic coast. To reach that city, however, the Germans would have to take the town of Mortain, just east of Avranches. This they did, but they failed to overrun the crucial high ground, Hill 317, from which U.S. troops had a panoramic view and could call in artillery fire and air support. Surrounded and taking heavy fire, the Americans

Artifacts

Maps of Normandy

With years to anticipate the invasion of German-occupied France, Overlord's planners made meticulous preparations—not only for the invasion of the beaches but also for the battle that would follow, as the Allies attempted to drive the Germans back across the Siegfried Line and into their own territory. This mapbook was issued to Allied officers and troops.

G.S.G.S. (MISC.) No. 77(2)
THROUGH-WAY TOWN PLANS OF
FRANCE
VOLUME 2
NORMANDY WEST OF THE SEINE

on Hill 317 held out for five days, fighting around the clock and incurring a 40% casualty rate. But they stopped the enemy: the Germans, halted at Mortain, never made it to Avranches.

NOW EVEN HITLER HAD TO ADMIT THAT RETREAT WAS HIS ONLY OPTION. ON Aug. 11, he authorized Von Kluge to begin an organized withdrawal eastward along the same 50-mile road he had traveled from Falaise just days before. But this time, Montgomery was waiting. Three days earlier, he had drawn up plans for Operation Totalize, in which British and Canadian troops would approach Falaise from the north, while Patton would swing around from the south and west, encircling the Germans. Soon most of the surviving German forces in northwest France were trapped inside this "Falaise Pocket" and were desperately trying to escape through a 15-mile-wide opening on its east side.

On Aug. 20, Patton and Montgomery's vanguards closed that gap at the towns of Trun and Chambois, 12 miles southeast of Falaise. Ten German divisions were trapped inside. Although as many as 20,000 Germans were able to slip through the still porous lines, more than three times that number were killed or captured within. The Battle of Normandy, which ended at Falaise, cost Hitler some 40 divisions. The Germans suffered losses of more than 240,000 killed or wounded and a nearly equal number captured. By Aug. 20, the Wehrmacht had ceased to exist as an effective fighting force in northwestern France.

Within the Falaise Pocket, the carnage was so intense that fighter pilots could smell the odor of death as they flew over the battlefield. When Eisenhower toured the scene later, he would write in his diary that the ground was so completely covered with corpses that for hundreds of yards in every direction it was impossible to avoid walking on them.

On Aug. 19, advance units of Patton's Third Army crossed the Seine. The road to Paris was now open, although Eisenhower diplomatically ordered Patton to slow his advance, while a French unit under General Jacques P. Leclerc marched from Falaise to enter the capital. The future was clear: once the German retreat from France had begun, both sides knew that it wouldn't stop, that there was no place for it to stop, until Hitler's army reached the Siegfried Line at Germany's border. The Führer would try one last roll of the dice, the desperate winter counteroffensive known as the Battle of the Bulge. But Adolf Hitler's days were numbered: once the sun rose on June 6, 1944, he would have 10 months to live. For now, the Allied troops could pause to celebrate the victory they had begun to win on D-day: after four years in chains, Paris prepared to welcome its liberators. ■

Mobile Warrior

As a young boy suffering from dyslexia, George Patton seemed an unlikely candidate to one day earn the nickname "Old Blood and Guts." Born into a wealthy California family in 1885, he was fragile, bookish and shy. But he was also spellbound by the stories of great battles he read in the Bible, history books and mythology texts. Patton's father egged him on with stories about relatives who had fought in the Civil War. The romance of arms inspired the young man, whom relatives described as "delicate," to transform himself into an idealized warrior and rugged leader.

Patton undertook a strict regimen of exercise and began to affect an extroverted, pugnacious personality, though he couldn't change his squeaky, high-pitched voice. He attended the Virginia Military Institute and graduated from West Point in 1909, after which he competed in the 1912 Olympics, placing fifth in the pentathlon. He helped chase Pancho Villa through Mexico, then served in World War I, in which he was wounded, promoted to colonel and awarded the Distinguished Service Cross.

Patton cultivated a reputation as an atypical officer who wrote poetry, studied history and believed in reincarnation. An evangelist for mobile warfare, he put theory into practice in World War II, leading victorious campaigns in North Africa, Italy and northern Europe. Preening in cavalry jodhpurs, a lacquered helmet and a uniform with padded shoulders, he insisted that his troops go into combat clean shaven and wearing ties. His emphasis on heroism led him to his great blunder, slapping two soldiers who had been hospitalized for combat fatigue. Mortally injured when his jeep collided with a truck in April 1945, he muttered, "This is a helluva way to die."

JUNE 26: The surrender of the Cherbourg garrison, commanded by Lieut. General Karl-Wilhelm von Schlieben, put the major port into Allied hands and helped the Allies make up for the loss of a Mulberry artifical harbor in the Great Storm of June 19-21

AUGUST 25, 1944

"I have never seen in any face such joy as radiated from the faces of the people of Paris this morning."
—TIME Reporter Charles C. Wertenbaker

Merci! Merci!

The Battle of Normandy ends in joy as the Allies enter Paris. A TIME reporter captures a magic moment

I HAVE SEEN THE FACES OF YOUNG PEOPLE IN LOVE AND the faces of old people at peace with their God. I have never seen in any face such joy as radiated from the faces of the people of Paris this morning. This is no day for restraint, and I could not write with restraint if I wanted to." The writer was Charles C. Wertenbaker; his cable from liberated Paris ran in TIME's issue dated Sept. 4, 1944. The account captures the emotions of that day with an immediacy impossible to duplicate. It continues, "Your correspondent and your photographer Bob Capa drove into Paris with eyes that would not stay dry, and we were no more ashamed of it than were the people who wept as they embraced us.

"We had spent the night at General [Jacques P.] Leclerc's command post, six miles from Paris on the Orléans-Paris road. Here the last German resistance outside Paris was being slowly reduced, while inside the city the Germans and the F.F.I. [Resistance] fought a bitter battle that had already lasted six days. Late in the afternoon a French cub plane flew in 50 yards above the Cathedral of Notre Dame, on the Ile de la Cité where the F.F.I. had its headquarters, and dropped a message which said simply: 'Tomorrow we come.'

"It was a fitting evening to precede the day of of Paris' liberation. It had rained all day while the French tanks maneuvered in the mud. Late in the afternoon the clouds blew away and the sun shone through a pale blue sky. Then the sun went down and quarter moon hung low above the plain. We stood in the twilight and discussed the news of the battle inside the city. It had started on the 19th and had never slackened in fury. By Thursday night the Resistance forces held not only the islands of Saint-Louis and La Cité but the Hotel de Ville, the Palais de Justice and the suburbs of Boulogne, Issy and Chatillon. The Germans held a large circular area bounded by the Eiffel Tower, the Invalides, the Gare du Quai-d'Orsay, the Place de la Concorde, the Madeleine and the Grand Palais.

HEROES' WELCOME: U.S. troops parade near the Hôtel de Ville, where snipers later opened fire, spoiling the party. Said TIME: "The women had smart clothes and cosmetics ... the supply of painted *filles* seemed ample to accommodate all soldiers interested in *amour*"

MOPPING UP: In the 9th arrondissement, near the Opera House, German officers are taken prisoner on Aug. 25. The Germans didn't contest the Allied entry into the city, preventing its ruin; in exchange, the Allies allowed most Germans to evacuate rather than surrender

HENRI CARTIER-BRESSON—MAGNUM PHOTOS

out the careless '20s Americans packed the cafés, the Dôme, the Coupole and the Select were locked, and so were the other restaurants. The people said there had been little food in Paris, and in the last weeks almost none. 'Are you bringing food to us?' they asked. We said the French had 300 trucks that would soon come to Paris with food. '*Merci! Merci! Merci!*'

"At the Gare Montparnasse, General Leclerc set up his headquarters and we drove on down the Boulevard over a street block the Germans had abandoned and into the Boulevard des Invalides. There was fighting in the streets ahead. A tank stopped before a house and for ten minutes pumped bullets into it. The tearing rattle of machine guns and the crackle of snipers' bullets sounded small against the echoing blast of the tanks' guns. French marines were trying to get into the

VIVE DE GAULLE! Amid a flotilla of admirers, Charles de Gaulle strides down the Champs Elysées. Though he commanded only a smallish army of Free French soldiers in 1944, De Gaulle insisted on being treated as a head of state, frustrating Eisenhower and other Allied leaders

BETTMANN/CORBIS

They also had strong points at the Gare d'Austerlitz, the Gare du Nord and the Porte d'Orléans.

"As darkness fell we spread our bedrolls beside the road to Paris and lay there under the starry sky and the low moon. Artillery sounded in the distance. At 6 o'clock in the morning the tanks began to move, and we followed as far as Antony, where a squad of Spanish Republicans stopped us. There was still enemy resistance ahead. Presently the tanks cleaned it up, and General Leclerc decided to go into Paris. It was 9 o'clock.

"We maneuvered our jeep just behind the General's armored car and drove fast toward the Porte d'Orléans. The people, who up to now had made small groups beside the road, suddenly became a dense crowd packed from the buildings to the middle of the street, where they separated to make a narrow line for the General's car to pass through. No longer did they simply throw flowers and kisses. They waved arms and flags and flowers; they climbed aboard the cars and jeeps embracing the French and us alike; they uttered a great mass cry of delight that swelled and died down and swelled to a greater height. They cried: '*Vive De Gaulle!*' and '*Vive Leclerc!*' But one word repeated over and over rose above all the other words. It was '*Merci! Merci! Merci!*'

"It was 9:35 when we entered the Avenue Aristide Briand, 9:40 when we passed through the Porte d'Orléans. This was Paris proper and, if such a thing were possible, the crowd grew thicker in the street. When the General's car stopped, they climbed up on it with their flowers and flags—Tricolors, Stars & Stripes, Union Jacks, Red flags with the hammer & sickle. Leclerc stood stiffly clutching his cane, never smiling, while the men in the armored car and in the jeeps behind took the crowds' embraces. Women held their children up to be kissed by the liberators, saying '*Merci, merci.*'

"At the Carrefour Raspail-Montparnasse, where through-

Chamber of Deputies, and some were being killed. I saw a bearded priest in a steel helmet hurrying down the street to give the last sacrament to one.

"The streets were full of people—Resistance groups armed with any old rifles, white-clad doctors and nurses carrying stretchers, and citizens old and young who, in spite of the danger, could not stay at home on this day. They gathered in crowds wherever something was happening, and everywhere something was happening. One crowd gathered around a German officer kneeling in the street praying for his life. A Resistance group was determined to shoot him on the spot, but three marines of the French Division got him free and took him prisoner.

"I went back to the jeep and set up my typewriter on the hood and began trying to write. Here on the the Boulevard des Invalides there was still much to see. Down the Boulevard a tank was shooting into the top story of a building where a sniper was making himself a nuisance. Up the Rue de Varenne to the right I could see a tank fighting a duel with a pillbox down a side street. Stone and plaster spattered from the buildings.

"Where there was not something to watch, there were people to talk to. All the people who saw the jeep came up with that look of utter joy on their faces. One woman brought me a sandwich, another a bottle of champagne. The one who had brought the sandwich came back to ask if I wanted a bath. I did." ∎

ROBERT CAPA—MAGNUM PHOTOS

A sniper attack at the Hôtel de Ville

Defying the Snipers

Even as the Allied armies entered Paris, a last remnant of foes put up a scattered, ineffective resistance. In the afternoon, crowds thronged the streets to welcome General Charles de Gaulle. Suddenly snipers opened fire on the crowded Place de la Concorde, sending civilians diving for cover. Most of the snipers were not Germans but Vichy militia and other fifth columnists who, unlike the German soldiers, could not give themselves up. As De Gaulle's procession approached the Cathedral of Notre Dame for a service of benediction, snipers opened fire. The scene was captured live by BBC radio correspondent Robert Reid:

"The General is being presented to the people. He is being received … [shouts, screams, a yell, then silence] … They have opened fire! … That was one of the most dramatic scenes I have ever seen … Firing started all over the place … General De Gaulle was trying to control the crowds rushing into the cathedral. He walked straight ahead into what appeared to me to be a hail of fire … But he went ahead without hesitation, his shoulders flung back, and walked right down the center aisle, even while the bullets were pouring about him. It was the most extraordinary example of courage I have ever seen … There were bangs, flashes all about him, yet he seemed to have an absolutely charmed life."

De Gaulle, TIME reported, continued his slow walk up the aisle. A *Te Deum* was playing from the organ where the snipers had hidden. After a brief ceremony, De Gaulle walked back down the aisle as calmly as he had gone up it. Said TIME: "Thus ended his first great public appearance in Paris. If there had been any doubt about his acceptance by the French people, this hour finished it."

Looking Back

On the anniversary of D-day, Presidents, paratroopers and privates gather to honor the heroes who gave the last full measure of devotion

AS THE YEARS PASS AND D-DAY RECEDES INTO LEGEND, the magnitude of its significance has not diminished; it has only increased. Here was a battle in which—for once amid history's murky ambiguities—there is no doubt about the antagonists: the Germans deserved to lose, the Allies to win. Here was a victory that absolutely transformed the course of world events. Here was a crusade that liberated a continent that had become a charnel house. And here are soldiers whose cause was just, whose courage is undeniable and whose legacy lives on.

The young men aged 18 and 20 who fought to win these beaches in 1944 will be 78 and 80 in 2004; their numbers are decreasing by the week. On the anniversaries of the event many of these aging veterans, their families and their admirers gather to commemorate their sacrifices and to honor their deeds. Visiting Normandy on the 40th anniversary of D-day, in 1984, President Ronald Reagan welcomed 62 of the Rangers who climbed Pointe du Hoc on the morning of June 6, 1944. "These are the boys of Pointe du Hoc," he said. "These are the champions who helped free a continent." And some of the men who were being hailed for their toughness took off their glasses to brush away tears. ■

REFLECTIONS: On June 6, 1969, the 25th anniversary of D-day, General Omar Bradley, 76, surveys Omaha Beach, some 160 yards from where he landed at 10:30 a.m. on June 7, the day after the invasion was launched. Bradley recalled that even the day after D-day, German artillery salvos were still roaring over the beach

LEAP OF FAITH: Veteran Bob Williams was one of 40 former paratroopers who re-lived D-day on its 50th anniversary by jumping into Normandy. Williams, said TIME photographer David Burnett, was moving briskly down the road, amid a cascade of "incoming": some 600 other parachutists who had joined the D-day veterans in the leap were landing all around him